T0286022

BUILT TO FINISH

HOW TO GO THE DISTANCE
IN BUSINESS AND IN LIFE

BUILT  TO
FINISH

STEVEN PIVNIK

GREENLEAF
BOOK GROUP PRESS

This publication is designed to provide accurate and authoritative information in regard to the subject matter covered. It is sold with the understanding that the publisher and author are not engaged in rendering legal, accounting, or other professional services. Nothing herein shall create an attorney-client relationship, and nothing herein shall constitute legal advice or a solicitation to offer legal advice. If legal advice or other expert assistance is required, the services of a competent professional should be sought.

Published by Greenleaf Book Group Press
Austin, Texas
www.gbgpress.com

Distributed by Greenleaf Book Group

For ordering information or special discounts for bulk purchases, please contact Greenleaf Book Group at PO Box 91869, Austin, TX 78709, 512.891.6100.

Design and composition by Greenleaf Book Group and Teresa Muñiz
Cover design by Greenleaf Book Group and Teresa Muñiz
Cover images used under license from ©stock.adobe.com/taitai6769; ©stock.adobe.com/snaptitude; ©stock.adobe.com/paru; ©stock.adobe.com/herraez; ©stock.adobe.com/wong sze fei, and ©shutterstock.com/Agnieszka Karpinska.

IRONMAN® and 70.3®, and their respective logos, are registered trademarks of World Triathlon Corporation in the United States and other countries. This independent publication has not been authorized, endorsed, sponsored or licensed by, nor has content been reviewed or otherwise approved by, World Triathlon Corporation, d/b/a The IRONMAN Group.

Publisher's Cataloging-in-Publication data is available.

Print ISBN: 979-8-88645-139-9

eBook ISBN: 979-8-88645-140-5

Audiobook ISBN: 979-8-88645-141-2

To offset the number of trees consumed in the printing of our books, Greenleaf donates a portion of the proceeds from each printing to the Arbor Day Foundation. Greenleaf Book Group has replaced over 50,000 trees since 2007.

23 24 25 26 27 28 29 30   10 9 8 7 6 5 4 3 2 1

First Edition

To my grandparents, who uprooted their entire family in search of a better life for us.

When you read this from heaven you'll see that your plan worked.

I'm eternally grateful to you.

NOTE ON TRIATHLON

The world of triathlon can be a little confusing if you aren't familiar with it. Made up of three parts—swim, bike, and run—the distances raced in triathlon vary.

One of the most challenging ones is the full-distance triathlon: 2.4 mile swim / 112 mile bike / 26.2 run. The most famous triathlons at this distance are produced by the World Triathlon Corporation and carry the brand name IRONMAN. Their brand guidelines, which I'm adhering to, are also very specific on how that name can be used, and so I use it sparingly in this book unless I'm referring to one of their specific races.

Other triathlon categories are:

Half distance: 1.2 mile swim / 56 mile bike / 13.1 mile run

Olympic distance: 0.93 mile swim / 24.8 mile bike / 6.2 mile run

Sprint: 0.5 mile swim / 12.4 mile bike / 3.1 mile run

In this book, wherever I use the word "triathlon" alone, I'm most often referring to a full-distance triathlon.

Pictures of all the adventures mentioned in this book can be found at stevenpivnik.com/blog. Search for the race or mountain name to get more details about the event, along with many photos.

CONTENTS

PROLOGUE

BUILT TO FINISH

"SHE DID A TRIATHLON?"

"Yeah, Steven, last week."

I felt somewhat surprised. I had thought that triathletes were this rare breed of superhumans with chiseled muscles and endless endurance. That is not to say that Rita wasn't in good shape, but it astounded me that she seemed to have just casually completed one of the most challenging and testing physical feats around, something I thought of as an exclusive Olympic event. Every now and again I'd turn on the television and see some athletic endurance event and quickly think there'd be no way I could do that. Maybe it was just my own self-limiting beliefs, or perhaps I just didn't really know what it took to complete a full triathlon. Either way, the fact that one of my employees had reached the finish line in one fascinated me.

As a middle-aged guy running a successful business, I spent most of my time focused on my family, my profession, and my friends. There wasn't much time for anything else. I wasn't a couch potato per se, but I wasn't a gym rat either. Skiing was my favorite sport, but we'd only get to the slopes a couple of times a year if we were lucky. I wasn't overweight or unhealthy, but I didn't celebrate beach season either. My dad bod and pasty complexion weren't exactly the stuff that dreams were made of.

Despite a normal, relatively healthy lifestyle, I often worried about my family genes. My grandparents and parents had all experienced some form or combination of cancer, high blood pressure, diabetes, and strokes. Talk about the short end of the stick when it comes to genetic health. That weighed on me often, as it does on many who lose the genetic lottery. But in response, I didn't do much other than regularly get physicals and try to follow an OK diet.

As I began to age and welcome the second half of my life, however, I looked around and wondered how I could improve my lifespan and avoid some of the diseases that ran in the Pivnik family. As you age, you often assess your life. I was no different. I felt like I needed some sort of adventure or to do something cool and interesting. So perhaps I was fated to learn that mere mortals can finish triathlons.

My brief conversation with my employees stayed with me over the weekend. I felt the tug to learn more. The following Monday, I learned about www.beginnertriathlete.com, where I found a large selection of races to compete in. It was that easy.

Just like that, I signed up, but I knew I couldn't just show up to the race. I was already looking forward to the commitment and the training, but there was still so much to digest.

I continued scouring the internet and quickly learned that I wasn't the only first-time shmuck endeavoring to run a race. One of the first things I researched was the race distance. I knew that a triathlon was a combination of three disciplines: running, biking, and swimming. But I hadn't the faintest idea which came first and how long each part lasted. It didn't take long to come to this harsh realization: In the Olympics, athletes swim one mile (1.5 km), bike twenty-five miles (40 km), and run six miles (10 km). Shit. This was no joke.

Looking at the event schedule, I found that some triathlons would be held near my hometown in New Jersey. In fact, one event was just an hour away from my house and located in Long Branch, right on the Jersey Shore. It was scheduled for September, four months out. It was a sprint distance triathlon, which is half the distance of an Olympic one. It seemed like a good place to start. *Baby steps*, I thought.

I was going to turn forty years old a week before the race and felt confident this would be a great way to bring in a new decade of my life. Over the next four months, I trained hard. Printing out a small daily training schedule to hold me accountable, each day I began to put time into swimming, biking, and/or running. It wasn't easy, especially the part in the pool. I wasn't half bad at running and biking. To some degree, these sports came naturally to me. With these two disciplines, I just needed to work on my form and pace. The pool was different. I didn't have the right form, had zero endurance, and I couldn't get my breathing down. A couple of laps left me completely spent.

That was a particularly tough road for me and my training. Once, while visiting the community pool, I nearly had a panic attack as I realized there was no way I could consecutively swim half a mile. That's thirty-two laps! The idea overwhelmed me. But I kept swimming. Two laps and I was exhausted. The next day, I swam the length of the pool three times. Right then and there I increased my output 50 percent. Even so, a lot of room for improvement remained. As consistent as my running and biking training seemed to be, the pool was my archnemesis. I didn't fear the water, and I wasn't incapable of swimming. It's just that it required tremendous physical output, often while I was fatigued from running and bike training.

I made myself complete the swim distance even though I had to stop and rest multiple times. The total distances in each discipline didn't seem overly challenging, but it was daunting to think I would have to complete each sport in turn, one right after the other. In more ways than one, I knew this would be a test of resilience and the human spirit.

As race day neared, I got excited to compete. We made it a family mini-vacation, and along with our two young girls, fourteen-year-old Stephanie and nine-year-old Rochelle, my wife, Larisa, and I drove to the Jersey Shore the day before the event. I wasn't sure if our daughters grasped what their crazy dad was trying to do, but it was nice that they wanted to come along for the ride, even if just for the perceived vacation.

The moment we hit the road, I began to get nervous, though I couldn't pinpoint exactly why. I'd done so much to prepare, and the next day it would be over. Maybe I was nervous that I wouldn't finish. My family was there, and I wanted to celebrate this win with them. Then my nervous energy gave way to another concern: What the hell would I eat the night before the race? I'd read a lot about pre-triathlon nutrition and encountered a lot of conflicting advice. But in the end, it's all about carbo loading and giving your body enough energy to burn before you embark on this beast of exertion. I think I settled on an oversized bowl of pasta, a little chicken, and a glass of red wine. I am quite the social drinker and love me a few cocktails. So, it was a feat in and of itself that I kept it to just one glass. I had a race to run.

Two Advil PM later, and I was out. The next morning started early, and I don't recall much detail leading up to the start of the race. I arrived on the beach, put on a wet suit, and nervously began to stretch and get my blood flowing. All the competitors were doing the same, but it seemed like it was taking a long time to get things started. I looked over to see the race officials and lifeguards huddling. I wondered what they were discussing, at least until I looked out at the ocean. It was noticeably choppy. Like, uncomfortably choppy. Dudes were surfing choppy. I eventually found out they were talking about canceling the swim. *No!* I had trained my ass off and wanted a shot at the entire experience. After a ten-minute conversation, they decided the show would go on. It was a great relief knowing we'd get the full challenge.

That relief was soon replaced with a little panic, but I steadied myself. I had swum in waves before and knew I could navigate these. Even so, I wasn't exactly Michael Phelps. Now, to make matters worse, there was about fifty yards of heavy chop I would have to navigate before things would level out. My bigger concern? That I would burn out on the swim and have nothing left for the bike and then run. The waves were high—really high. This was no joke. I could only imagine what Larisa was thinking: *Motorcycle accidents didn't kill Steven, but triathlon did.*

On this September morning, the competitors edged up to the start line just feet away from the chilly Jersey Shore ocean water. We waited for the sound of the signal to start. The gun went off, and we all ran into the water, half flailing and half trying to navigate the crazy waves. About a hundred of us were all trying to get through the chop. While swallowing ocean water and avoiding flying fists and kicking feet, I eventually found my rhythm.

Kick. Push. Glide. Breathe. Repeat. Kick. Push. Glide. Breathe. Repeat. Things got much easier after I survived the breaking surf. I managed to conserve energy, create personal space, and weather my biggest concern—the swim. As my feet met the wet sand, I found immediate relief. Jugs of water awaited better prepared athletes in their transition spot, offering some respite from the harsh salt water that infiltrated their mouths, noses, and beneath their goggles into their eyes. None awaited this rookie, so relief from the salt would have to wait. Adding to the lack of experience, I got stuck as I tried to rip off my wet suit. On that hot shore day, it stuck to me like glue. It took longer than expected, but I finally got into my biking gear and took off. The bike leg was, thankfully, uneventful. I knew it would be. As I completed the twelve-mile ride, I dismounted my bike and put on my running shoes. *Homestretch*, I thought.

Out of nowhere, almost immediately, a stabbing pain hit my side. Triathletes call this "stitches"—shooting cramps. Great. I slowed to a jog and eventually to a steady walk. After navigating them for a few hundred yards or so, they eventually subsided, and I picked up my pace a bit. Things quickly leveled out for me, and I began to feel like I might reach the finish line.

The rest of the run passed with ease. I had been running on adrenaline but then I literally hit my stride during the final mile. As I turned one corner, off the boardwalk and back to Seven Presidents Park, I saw the big, checkered flag that signaled the race finish. I began to practically sprint in its direction, running toward my cheering family. Before me, I saw dozens of participants finishing the race. As I crossed the line, I looked back toward the remaining competitors, and with that glance, a total sense of relief filled me. I hadn't told my family, but my only goal had been to finish the race before one other person.

Though I was covered in sweat, ocean water, and whatever filth had been kicked up, Rochelle ran up to me with outstretched arms. I was hesitant to hug her, but she made it abundantly clear that she didn't care about the sweat and dirt. It was a wonderful, endearing moment. I'll never forget her words: "I don't care how wet you are, Daddy. I'm so proud, I want to hug you!"

After the race, we drove back to the hotel, where I showered, and we checked out. I was on cloud nine. We packed up and hit the road for the short drive back home. My mind began to wander, thinking about what I had just accomplished. It felt surreal, something I had spent months building up to. I could check the box, a first-time triathlon. As that elation wore off, something else replaced it: a desire to do it again. That surprised me as I initially thought this would be a one-and-done experience and I would be off to chase the next shiny object.

Back at home, I sat comfortably on the living room couch and emailed my co-workers. "I just got home from my first triathlon and made it to the finish line. It was amazing. And, I didn't finish last. I can't thank you enough for all your support and starting me out on this journey." With a large grin, I began to review the weekend's work emails. An hour later, a reply from Rita popped up on the screen. It read: "Great job, Steven. I knew you could do it. I am sure we will see you in Kona one day."

Kona? As in Hawaii? What does that have to do with triathlons?

Immediately, I pulled up Google and started to search for "Triathlon, Kona, Hawaii." Numerous sites and YouTube videos referenced something called the IRONMAN® World Championship, apparently the longest-distance triathlon event. It originated in Hawaii, and the yearly IRONMAN World Championship has been held there since 1978, an annual culmination of the qualification races throughout the entire world. Quickly, I realized that this was the best of the best, a total dream for any triathlete. And there I was, Steven from New Jersey, just having completed his first sprint triathlon. Needless to say, I was a long way from becoming a full-distance triathlete and racing in Kona.

But something special happened in that moment. Just like a seed had inadvertently been planted in my mind to complete my first triathlon, it had just happened again. The more I read about the event, and the more I watched motivational YouTube videos, the more I wanted to find a way to be a part of it. As you can imagine, a remarkable amount of effort and dedication are required to finish a race that long, let alone qualify for the World Championship, but it became my obsession. Over the next two years, I started to slowly increase my distances and run race after race. From half-marathons to full marathons to Olympic-distance triathlons to half-distance triathlons, something came over me and I fell completely in love with the sport and the healthy lifestyle.

I improved my running, biking, and swimming times, along with increasing their respective distances and my overall endurance. In many ways, I transformed my body and mind into an endurance machine. Persistence, discipline, resilience, and drive became the bedrocks for my success as an athlete just as they had been the bedrocks for my success in and out of the boardroom for many years. Day after day, week after week, month after month, the dream of completing more and more triathlons became my life. Eventually, I ramped up to full-distance triathlons, which encompass a 2.4-mile (1.9 km) swim, a 112-mile (90 km) ride, and a 26.2-mile (42 km) run.

Steven the businessman and CEO became Steven the Triathlete. I felt humbled by the accomplishment, using my same work ethic in business to train like a madman. Now, as I write these final introductory words, I stand just months from recognizing a dream that started with an innocent conversation at work. Kona is in plain view, and I have qualified for the event after completing one grueling triathlon after another, after another. It is something I earned and one of my greatest accomplishments, along with successfully exiting my business only 13 months prior. But how I got here is almost as special as my arrival at its doorsteps.

That story begins nearly fifty years ago in Eastern Europe. Today, I am a very different man, but one who still uses his childhood lessons to build success in and out of the boardroom. I have lived a limitless life, one that recognizes that you can accomplish nearly anything, even miracles, because anything is possible if you believe and desire it enough.

EMBRACING THE GRIND

THE GRIND. WE HAVE ALL BEEN THERE. For me it sometimes begins with the early morning alarm clock and knowing I have to get out of bed, put one foot in front of the other, and get to the day's workout. Sometimes it's the infamous mile twenty of a marathon where all I want to do is curl up in a fetal position and go to sleep.

I've completed the New York City Marathon eight times. Running over the Verrazzano-Narrows Bridge with its incredible ocean and Manhattan skyline views is exhilarating. The crowds up Fourth Avenue in Brooklyn provide amazing encouragement. The various neighborhoods in Queens highlight the diversity of this incredible city I'm running through and provide some needed distraction from the lactic acid building up in my legs. Entering Manhattan via the very steep Ed Koch Queensboro Bridge, which most locals call the Fifty-Ninth Street Bridge, is super taxing on the body, and many have to walk this section of the race. The reward is the cheering crowd on the upper east side which gives everyone a bit of a second wind to keep running.

And then, when you think you're so, so close, you enter the Bronx and the dreaded twenty-mile mark. Many athletes describe a marathon as two races. The first twenty miles and the last six. And that last six miles you have to force yourself to keep going when your body is bone tired; one foot in front of the other when it feels impossible to do so. There is no better depiction of the grind.

The dictionary defines a *grind* as hard, dull work. It's the type of effort that doesn't lead to any glory or success but is an absolutely necessary evil if you want to accomplish anything. We don't celebrate the grind, but the grind is where character is built and winning occurs. Anything that has real value results from the grind. The effort, the dedication, the determination, and the resilience. It is the perseverance that greases the wheel of success. We are where we are because of the grind, and we aren't where we want to be because we need to grind it out even more. Sometimes, the grind is the product of an incredible amount of discomfort. Other times, it is a slow, steady burn that follows us through any endeavor or goal. If you aren't grinding, then you aren't trying. Whether it be competing and finishing one of my many endurance challenges and races, or building my business which I eventually sold, I was always grinding in one way or another.

My life, a proverbial grind, has humble origins. Nothing glorious, just an Eastern European Jewish family living in the former Soviet Union, USSR. I was born in a port town called Odessa, part of what is now the Ukraine. A multigenerational Soviet, I came into this world during the height of the Cold War and at the hand of Leonid Brezhnev's rule. We were extremely isolated, and the Communist party attempted to have total ideological control. While my family wasn't particularly religious, we were practicing Jews and celebrated the High Holidays and other important customs.

Anti-Semitism was very much alive in the USSR when my family lived there. It was an uncomfortable place to be, and my parents and grandparents wanted more for us. Once, a woman approached my grandmother at a local convenience store and broke a glass bottle over her head, yelling "Dirty Jew" as she ran away. Despite our feeling of home and community, my grandfather and father made the difficult decision to leave in search of a better, more stable life. So began the grind of packing up our family and all our worldly possessions and then moving to the United States of America. We received the assistance for this daunting undertaking from an organization called the New York Association for New Americans (NYANA). They sponsored Eastern European Jews emigrating from particularly anti-Semitic and challenging places. The USSR was one of those places.

We left Odessa in the middle of the night and took a train to Vienna, Austria. After a short stop in Vienna, we traveled to Rome. Upon arriving there, we awaited our final paperwork to head to the United States. We started our search for a place to live by visiting building after building, inquiring about the availability of an apartment to rent. The only response we received: *"Non adesso." Why are they discriminating against folks from Odessa?* we wondered. Only later that day did we learn that *"non adesso"* meant "not now" in Italian, meaning there was no vacancy in the building for anyone, regardless of whether or not they were from Odessa. While I didn't know it at the time, my parents' courage was setting the table for overcoming a great deal of adversity in my own future. My family endured the grind countless times on our journey to America, starting with that search to put a roof over our heads in Italy. The grind, as I would later learn, is part of any journey of meaning. It is the lubrication that helps you shift gears and climb over the steep hills ahead.

Eventually, we found an apartment in Rome, where we lived for nearly six months, waiting and waiting. My father took this time to learn English, along with working various jobs to save some money for the journey ahead. From a young age, I spoke to my father in English, one of his requirements when we communicated. I didn't know it at the time, but he was clearly preparing me for our arrival to the United States. He knew I didn't have a chance if I couldn't speak the native tongue.

While in Rome, the immigration authorities offered us a few other choices for our final destination. From Australia to Israel to America, we didn't have the faintest idea which would be a good fit for us. They offered us a couple of options within America as well: Ohio and New York. We already knew one family that had made it to New York, so we picked the Big Apple to start an entirely new whirlwind of a grind. We packed everything, *again*, flying from Rome to JFK Airport, and then we were shuttled to Brighton Beach in Brooklyn, known as the Russian speaking capital of the United States to this day.

If my family was struggling when they arrived in the United States, they didn't ever once let us, the children, feel it. That was crucial to my development. I always felt safe and comfortable. If the grind was wearing my parents down, they didn't let us see it. We never shared in the pain and suffering, left to be innocent and fun-loving kids.

I needed to use these same tactics when running my company. As a leader I couldn't show fear or uncertainty during rough times. It was always a positive attitude and a continuous rallying cry to the troops, even during the months when I had no clue how I was going to make payroll.

America was different. Very different. We basically woke up in a new country, with no money and hardly any way to understand the native culture or language, and we started an entirely new type of grind. NYANA secured us a gorgeous duplex apartment in Coney Island but now it was up to us to make ends meet. To survive. Still, my family knew that we had made the right choice. There was just so much freedom, in nearly everything we could do. The freedom of choice was a remarkably new experience for any immigrant coming from the USSR, and we were no different.

That freedom had its positives and negatives. For example, we could believe what we wanted, do what we wanted, say what we wanted, and pursue the dreams that we wanted to dream. In many ways, it was nearly a new lease on life. But we also had a little bit of catching up to do. As a family, we had lost so much time living under the thumb of the Soviet government. Just think what it might have felt like to get circumcised when you were five years old instead of the traditional eight days old, which is exactly what happened to me since that was part of traditional Judaism but forbidden where I was born. That was a day I wouldn't soon forget. Ouch!! Looking back, the gift of choice was clearly a remarkable opportunity, but I wish we could have made some of these choices a little bit earlier in my life.

My father started off working blue collar jobs, first as an air conditioning serviceman, then as an automobile mechanic. Eventually, he worked in a collision repair shop, and he built his own customer base, starting a shop of his own. That is what I credit my entrepreneurial spirit to—my father setting a great example from a young age. He was a salt of the earth type of man, willing to do the type of backbreaking work most people aren't particularly interested in. From a young age in America, I witnessed him wake up early every day, work every single Saturday, come home late, and never once take a sick day.

He worked hard outside of the house, and my mother was always there to provide for us at home. She was ever present, a housewife, and always there to raise me and my sister, Angela. Angela was made in Italy and born a few months after we arrived in the US. My grandfather got a job as a bus driver for an Orthodox school in Borough Park, Brooklyn. He had that job for many years until he retired. My grandmother accepted a job at a candy factory, and I always imagined the *I Love Lucy* conveyor belt scene when she departed for work. It clearly wasn't that glorious, but I have fond memories of her returning home with a small bag of treats for us.

Eventually, my grandparents got an apartment of their own, just seven blocks away. Having them so close was wonderful; they were a constant example of love and mentorship. They had a rock-solid relationship, the matriarch and patriarch of the family. My parents were no different. When my sister got a little older, my mom joined the working class again and got a job as a nurse. When my parents weren't working, they enjoyed going out and spending time with friends. On multiple occasions, they'd drop us kids off at my grandparents' after work on Friday and we wouldn't see them again until Sunday evening. It didn't matter much to us as we loved our grandparents.

I fondly remember spending almost every weekend in the summer at the beach across the street from where they lived. We would arrive early to get oceanfront spots. I spent countless hours in the waves of the Atlantic Ocean. That is where I became comfortable in the water. My grandmother would leave in the early afternoon to start preparing dinner. My grandparents' apartment faced the beach; around mealtime, we'd look for a large white towel hanging from their fifth-story window, signaling to us that dinner was ready.

My schooling began at a local yeshiva, where I studied Hebrew, Bible studies, and other Judaism-related topics in addition to all the standard US subjects. The strenuous curriculum and long days really took it out of you. I was a relatively good student, but at times I found my mind drifting. It was hard enough to come to America and learn a new language, but to stack Hebrew on top of it seemed like an unmanageable task. But I did my best. My fellow students and I made our studies into a fun competition. We were all competitive and worked hard to see who could get the best grades.

I excelled in secular studies, specifically math and science. I had passionate teachers in these areas, and their excitement inspired each student in the classroom. That made it easy to learn, and I fell in love with these subjects. Though I was nerdy and not one for sports, I found a group of kids who shared similar interests, which made it quite easy to fit in. It didn't matter if I was the most popular kid on the block as I found peace in being around other kids who loved what I loved.

But school wasn't always easy for me. At times, I struggled with Jewish studies, and this caused me a great deal of anxiety. While I did my best, I nearly had a complete meltdown on at least one occasion. One day, with my bookbag on my back, I decided to run away from home instead of going to school. Thankfully, I didn't make it far. As I roamed the streets of Brighton Beach, my grandmother's sister found me, scolded me, and walked me back to my apartment. I don't know what the hell I was thinking. Who runs away from home and school with nothing but their bookbag? Only amateurs don't strategically plan an escape route.

Outside of school, I loved playing with computers. Eventually, I persuaded my father to purchase a Commodore 64, one of the first and most basic consumer-use computers. After bringing that home from a consumer electronics store called Crazy Eddie on Coney Island Avenue, you couldn't get me away from it. I spent hours upon hours tinkering with it, writing programs. My affinity for computers began to take root at this time. When I wasn't in front of the computer, I enjoyed reading magazines and riding bikes. It was a gift to be so close to Coney Island, which, at the time, was shaping into its modern-day version. The boardwalk was bustling and a great place for people watching. After school, a group of us would ride our bikes to Coney Island's carnival-like backdrop where we would grab hot dogs and watch families partake in the joys of our surroundings. The boardwalk was a long stretch, maybe two or three miles, and a perfect place to ride our bikes until the sun set. Little did I know I would be spending a lot more of my life on the saddle.

An ice-skating rink sat smack-dab in the middle of Coney Island; my family and I would visit it often. We'd also visit the local bowling alley and after a few hours of knocking down pins, go to a local dinner spot called Beefsteak Charlie's. I always looked forward to the weekends as they involved spending time with our grandparents or our parents taking us to the rink or the bowling alley. This was a remarkable time, especially compared to what we left in the USSR. That was an oppressive culture, and America was a breath of fresh air, allowing us to enjoy our lives and freedom of choice without facing violence or constant harassment.

There were just so many differences between the USSR and the US. In a society of pure communism, the government controls nearly everything. Imagine waiting in a long line just to get your weekly rations. There is no abundance. No one gets any more than what the government decides is appropriate. We had to carefully consider nearly every word that came out of our mouth and had to practice Judaism in complete secrecy. Arriving in the US was a welcomed shock to our existence. Just the simple fact that we had free speech to say what we wanted was a truly remarkable change. The USSR was a very sad, gray place. It was readily apparent that my family had made not just the objectively right decision but also the safest one for all of us.

We loved our freedom, as a family unit and as Jews living in the US. Back in the USSR, it was unheard of for a young Jewish boy to have a bar mitzvah, the Jewish ceremony celebrating coming of age. But in the US, I was approaching my thirteenth birthday, practicing daily to prepare for my own bar mitzvah. It was just one of the many gifts we received by immigrating to the United States. But we also experienced significant loss leading to this special time in my life. My grandmother had been sick with colon cancer, and she passed away just three weeks before my bar mitzvah. As they say in New York, the show must go on. Following Jewish tradition to honor the recent loss of a loved one, we didn't have any music or other celebratory traditions at my party. Rather, we were mostly quiet. We lit the traditional fourteen candles and had dinner. It was strange to bring all our friends and family together to this incredibly somber environment. Losing my grandmother was really my first experience with loss, and it hit hard. She was a wonderful woman, the matriarch of my family, and forever missed.

As I entered high school, I quickly noticed a significant wealth disparity between my family and the families of others who attended my school. This wouldn't be the last time I didn't feel like I fit. It would happen again when I started my business, Binary Tree, and then when I raced my first full-distance triathlon. In each of those occasions, I found myself looking around and feeling like an imposter. However, the more I grinded it out and found greater success, the more I realized that I not only belonged, I also had what it takes to succeed.

My father, a remarkable man, helped to reduce the noticeable differences between me and my classmates by purchasing me a car. It was a

$300 Oldsmobile Omega. It wasn't glamorous at all, with its stained cloth seats, rickety transmission, manual windows, and the softest blowing A/C you could imagine. I'd often pull into the parking lot and find myself next to a brand-new Porsche or Ferrari as many of my classmates came from substantial money. An extremely large Syrian-Jewish community was emerging in Brooklyn, and for whatever reason, many of these people were incredibly rich. They weren't shy with their wealth and often put it on full display as they walked the school hallways.

Once, as I eagerly returned to school from spring break, wearing my normal clothes that had carried me the previous season, I was greeted with, "Hey, Steven, why are you still wearing your winter clothes?" All the rich kids in their new summer colors laughed out loud as I sheepishly sat and sank into my chair. I was hardly ever the target of bullies, but you could feel and see the wealth disparity. I don't think they knew that I was able to sit among them because of an immigrant scholarship the school granted.

I was a hard worker in and out of school and always had a job. Before I could even get my official working papers that enabled employment, my father found me a job pumping gas at a neighborhood station. The owner, my father's buddy, would pay me cash at the end of each week. Eventually, I learned how to do oil changes and run the cash register. The following summer I had a newspaper route, which I loved because it meant more time on my bicycle. By the time I became a senior, the extra Jewish studies were cutting into my budding social life, so I left the yeshiva and switched to public school. That gave me an even greater capacity to pursue jobs and side hustles. I became a cashier at a local supermarket called Waldbaum's. My knack for computers gave me the edge to become the quickest cashier on the floor. I exhibited such talent that the manager eventually put me at the head of training for all new cashiers and later promoted me to front end runner. That's supermarket lingo for "middle management." Each of these humble jobs instilled a strong work ethic in me. It doesn't take a glamorous job to build character. Sometimes it is the most mundane and simple tasks, done with great pride, that really help to develop your ability to grind.

But I still wasn't making enough money, so I took a second job as a Domino's Pizza delivery driver. Delivering pizzas wasn't terribly difficult, and I enjoyed driving around town and seeing people's pleasure when I showed up with a nice hot pizza. One Super Bowl Sunday, I pulled up to a house to deliver a bunch of pies and sodas. The door opened to reveal, to my horror, the same classmate that had made fun of my clothes. Even worse, I heard many familiar voices coming from inside. Here I was working my ass off while everyone else was enjoying the game. That wasn't particularly pleasant, but moments like this taught me the importance of the grind.

Some moments trigger a strong emotional response. Often, that emotion can define a new deep physiological foundation from which future desires, actions, and goals emanate. It can be as extreme as physical abuse at an early age that triggers an "I'll never be hurt again" mentality. My feelings of embarrassment and inferiority triggered a subliminal desire to climb to the top.

When my father's auto body business went bust, he still figured out ways to support our family. He bought into a limo company and began driving at all hours of the day. I began chipping in some of my earnings to help support our family and kept the rest to spend on my own personal hobbies. This was really the first time I felt the grind. I was working hard and now had to share in the household responsibilities in a very different way. I didn't mind, but it felt like I was growing up much quicker than most of my peers.

My family taught me a tremendous amount about the grind. In many ways, they helped forge the rock-solid foundation that has served me for most of my life. You learn the grind from watching the grind. When I was attempting my first mountain summit, the top was in sight, but I was exhausted and running on fumes. The lead guide told me to watch his boots and place my boots with each step in his tracks. Watching him continue to ascend, and slowly following in his footsteps got me to the top.

From the difficult path of immigration to building a life in America to working day in and day out to take control of our new freedom and give the next generation an opportunity to create something bigger and better— it was all an endless grind.

Little did I know, the real grind was about to really begin.

Key Takeaways

- The grind can be tough, but anything that has real value results from effort, dedication, determination, and resilience. The grind is perseverance.

- There's opportunity for success in being willing to do the type of backbreaking work most people choose not to do.

- Give the people that you want to see thrive a safe place in which to grow.

- Embracing the grind not only propels you forward, it also leaves a blueprint for other hard workers to follow.

THE BEEKMAN FIVE

I'VE LEARNED THE HARD WAY that your first attempt at a new endeavor will be suboptimal at best and may result in a complete failure, but it will be a great learning experience. During my first attempt at an ultramarathon, my rookie mistakes were almost comical. I didn't research that the Monument Valley 50k terrain was a mile above sea level and required a couple of days of acclimatization. I figured that out after it got pretty hard to breathe after only a quarter mile of running. I also didn't know that about half of the course would be in sand, unlike the pretty pictures of hardpack dirt trails where the old Marlboro Man commercials were filmed. Not only is it harder to run in, but there is also special footwear available to reduce sand accumulation in your sneakers. I did not have this nor any of the other gear that many more experienced racers did. While I suffered mightily through that event, I knew that it was a huge learning experience, and I would be back for other ultras better prepared.

Toward the end of high school, I began to consider my next move. My parents weren't strong on academics and didn't demand that I attend college. Certainly, this was an out-of-the-ordinary perspective, but it offered me more options (and opportunities to misstep) than many of my counterparts had. Luckily, I felt a strong desire to pursue a traditional education. I applied and was accepted to Polytechnic University, a great technical school in Brooklyn. I was elated, but my parents quickly burst my bubble when they said they couldn't afford to send me there.

So, I ended up attending Baruch College, a state school in Manhattan. It hardly compared to Polytech, but it was really my only opportunity for a higher education. College was strange. It seemed that everyone else had a clear path and detailed plan. Not me. While my friends were set on becoming lawyers, accountants, doctors, and pharmacists, I didn't know what my next move would be. However, I was still pretty good with computers, and I continued to tinker away.

During this time, my mother found out about a nine-month computer programming course in downtown Manhattan that guaranteed job placement upon completion. A real job would allow me to chip in and help support my family further and begin to build toward bigger and better opportunities. This course proved to be one of the most important discoveries up to that point in my life.

It was called The Beekman Five—a name that sounds like an elite group of superheroes. It was actually called something else, but it was located on 5 Beekman Street so that is what everyone called it. I don't even remember the actual name. I was excited about the opportunity but still wanted my father's approval. Though he never really pushed me in a specific academic direction, he really wanted to see his son get a bona fide college degree. Not understanding the potential in the computer field, he was not happy when I told him I preferred this course over attending college, but he begrudgingly agreed to let me drop out.

I can only imagine other similarly situated families would push hard for their child to remain in school. I often think about where I would be today if my father had done the same. The experience of immigrating gave us such a different view of the world. We appreciated the endless opportunities in our new country, and as part of that, we had to welcome in the variety of choices we had available to us.

Even so, someone had to pay tuition, and that someone would be me. I started driving his limo at night to earn the money. I really enjoyed the course and quickly realized I was clearly the most accomplished programmer in the room.

Beekman Five was well ahead of its time, a computer programmer's dream well before computers became as popular as they are today. The world had hardly entered the Golden Age of computers, and the PC generation was still a decade away. Nonetheless, we used mainframes and learned programming languages called COBOL, VSAM, JCL, and CICS. This new stuff came relatively easy to me due to endless hours geeking out with my Commodore 64. That gave me a decisive advantage over my fellow classmates and eventually led me to get the first job among my cohorts at a little publishing company called *Reader's Digest* with a starting salary of $19,000 a year. That was a huge amount for me.

I thank my parents for recognizing my entrepreneurial spirit and creating and supporting what others might have called a horrible idea. In many ways, I was lucky to have parents who didn't subscribe to the traditional American ideals.

Reader's Digest was an incredibly popular form of print media in the 1970s and '80s. I was living with my parents in Brooklyn and commuting to Pleasantville, Westchester, which was more than ninety minutes each way, and I leaned heavily on a brash radio host named Howard Stern, who helped get me through those grueling traffic-filled drives. Add in a little caffeine and soda, and I was good to go. It was quite a change to go from school to a professional environment, and I was awkward at best in my efforts to fit in. I still recall my first day, getting the nickel tour from the recruiter who landed the job for me. As she asked me to walk her out of the building on my first day, I turned to her and said, "I'm not sure what the schedule is like here, but what time are the breaks and how long are they?"

Almost laughing, she said, "Honey, this is *Reader's Digest*, not the supermarket you worked at. You can take breaks when you need them. Welcome to the real world."

In many ways, I felt as if I had arrived at a place for which I was destined. *Reader's Digest* had a world-record-setting customer billing program, and I was part of the team writing the code for it—60,000 lines of code, which is massive, was the foundation for the millions of invoices the company sent out each week. Our team was tasked with continuously updating the code based on requirements handed down by various business units. We tested all programming changes and peer reviewed them prior to scheduling the program to run so that customer records could be updated, and invoices could be sent out.

Rinse and repeat. Rinse and repeat. These kind of mundane but important tasks are extremely important to help you develop the muscles you need to thrive. Talk to most any entrepreneur, and they will often tell you that they did anything and everything to build their business. Few have the resources and ability to hire employees or pass these responsibilities to others. They have to do it themselves, and that helps them to learn the business and appreciate their origins. I was no different. Though it could be repetitive at times, I also really enjoyed the complexity of the work. It was remarkable to work on such a detail-oriented and involved project. While I followed protocol, I also spent additional time outside of normal work hours tinkering, toying, and attempting to improve the code. I figured my dedication and additional effort would pay off, but instead, it manifested one of the greatest lessons I would ever learn about following protocol. Late at night and early in the mornings, I was working on code. One evening, I was so excited about the enhancement I engineered that I eagerly moved it into production without going through the regular peer-review programming process to ensure there would be no adverse impact on the customer profiles.

The following morning, I was super eager to see the results of my discovery and looked up various reports that were produced when the program ran overnight. Quickly, I realized the numbers were way off and that something very odd had occurred. After reviewing my code with a clear head, I quickly figured out that I had, inadvertently, introduced a bug into it. I had made a complete rookie mistake consisting of omitting one single command. When I realized this, I faced an extremely difficult decision: Do I put my head down, pretend as if it never happened, and hope for the best, or do I come clean? My moral upbringing prevailed; it was no decision at all. Practically shaking, I walked into my manager's office and came clean. I told her I made a mistake, screwed up the code, and introduced a bug. It didn't take but forty-five minutes for a swarm of execs to descend on our area, frantically walking in and out of my office as if it were ground zero in some sort of nuclear explosion.

As I watched, they hopped into motion. Eventually, the team decided to restore all the customer data from the latest backup, repair my bug, and rerun the program. An enormous trickle-down effect resulted. Bills went out late and computing costs went through the roof. I would later learn that my mistake had cost the company several million dollars in additional IT costs and delayed billing. I felt horrible. As I sat in my office with my head between my hands wondering when God would end it all for me, my manager walked in. I looked up, prepared to be fired. She closed the door, sat down in front of me, calm and collected.

It was likely clear as day how incredibly upset I was, and if tears weren't yet actually streaming down my face, I felt like they were about to flow at any minute. She remained calm, even stoic. "Steven, I can tell you are upset. You're a young man, and you have your entire career in front of you. I'm not going to ruin it because of one mistake. So, Steven, please do not do that again." I was shocked. Looking up from my desk, even closer to tears, I practically hugged her and thanked her for the remarkable grace she offered me. It was hardly deserved but absolutely appreciated. That second chance proved to be an important break in my life. Had she just fired me, like about 99 percent of bosses likely would have, I don't know how I would have recovered. Instead, she instilled a level of compassion in me and taught me a valuable lesson that I would later use with my own employees.

In the business world, mistakes will inevitably happen. When they do, it's paramount to acknowledge them, apologize, and then bend over backwards to rectify them. In most cases, the remedy will come at your own expense. Smart customers will notice the remorse and hard work of your corrective actions. They'll remember your efforts and commitment to fix the problem more than the original problem itself.

The biggest example of this I can remember is from a project at Apple Vacations. My company's software product erroneously migrated the

CEO's email data to a lower level employee's mailbox. We had to pull a couple of all-nighters to fix the issue that had caused this. I had to pull the owner card, appear on-site, and swear to executives that this would never happen again. To our bewilderment the same issue reoccurred, and I had to fall on my sword yet again. As they say, the third time's the charm, and we finally fixed the issue once and for all. The project ended up being a great success with many valuable lessons learned.

Back at *Reader's Digest*, I was establishing some good friendships. One day, I learned that one of my friends had a minor motorcycle mishap and decided to sell his ride because it had been slightly damaged. Hardcore enthusiasts of any kind don't deal well with imperfections. With his eye on a new model, he was selling the scratched Honda Interceptor 500 for a steal at only $1,000. I did not have a penny saved but did have a passion for motorbikes. I was so excited about this bargain that I borrowed the money at a crazy interest rate so I could take advantage of the opportunity. When you want something bad enough, you'll often justify creative ways to go about getting it. My adrenaline addiction was now officially on, and it would manifest itself in more motorcycles in the future and other activities in the years to come.

I spent the next year and a half of my life at *Reader's Digest*. In many ways, it was one of the most important parts of my young life. So many firsts occurred, including getting serious with my girlfriend, Larisa, whom I would later marry. When I'd first met her several years prior, I was immediately attracted to her and began asking her out. I gave up after several denials, but fate turned in my favor when she asked me out on my eighteenth birthday. It seems as if she hasn't left my side since. From job to job, potential career to career, crazy races to even crazier adventures, she has been there through it all while also pursuing a career of her own.

After gaining a great deal of experience and learning a few valuable lessons along the way, I left *Reader's Digest* for a job at Mercantile Stores, which was like a smaller version of Macy's. Mercantile hired me to join a team building a new automated inventory replenishment system, which was very cutting edge at the time. Looking around, it seemed like I had made it to some version of the big leagues, surrounded by college grads, MBAs, Arthur Andersen consultants, and other super-polished professionals. I was regularly working with several experienced colleagues and showing my development and acumen for the job. Around the same time, the world began to see the release of personal computers, and it was no longer uncommon for a household to own an IBM PC or one of many popular compatibles as they were called. They were extremely expensive, and there was no way I could afford one. What I could do though, with the help of a little training and advice, was build my own.

I took up this new hobby and began to source parts from local stores and mail order catalogues. It was an amazing experience, one that would continue for years to come. With the dual knowledge of mainframe programming and my burgeoning skills for PC programming, I was equipped with all I needed to make a splash in the industry. I was getting better and better trained, so much so that Merrill Lynch in midtown Manhattan offered me a position. My tedious ninety-minute driving commute was replaced with an easy subway ride. To say that job was boring at best would be a great understatement. It looked good on a resume, but I didn't have the patience to work on what became a very unexciting back-office project and gave my notice just shy of ninety days in.

While I was contemplating my next professional move, my next personal move was clearly in sight. I proposed to Larisa, and we were married in 1991 at a Jewish Community Center and catering hall in

Brooklyn. Earlier that year, I had started my next job at a freight container shipping company called Sealand, where I worked on worldwide logistics shipping systems. There, I ran into someone I recognized from high school. When I asked him if he was a programmer too, he replied, "No, I'm a software engineer." *What an ass*, I thought. We didn't speak again, although I'm sure I've used that title a few times going forward to describe what I do.

While I really enjoyed my day job, I found a greater reward in my night and weekend activities. I was continuing to build my PC skills, and I utilized them to find a little side hustle helping smaller companies develop computer programs to run their businesses. A light bulb went off in my head. One of my first clients was a fashion manufacturing company, and if they needed my services, why wouldn't others?

In response, I opened the Yellow Pages and found fifty other companies in the same industry. All of them were up and down Seventh Avenue, also known as Fashion Avenue, in New York City. I created a manual cut and paste letter-writing campaign, where I mailed each company a basic flyer advertising my business and the benefits it would bring them. I offered them a computer program that could handle invoicing and inventory management. I sent the mailers off and held my breath. And . . . nothing! Literally not one single phone call. I was done before I could even get out of the gate. Complete and utter failure. Thank God I had a day job because my first shot at being an entrepreneur was a catastrophic failure. About the same time, I learned that my current company, Sealand, was being acquired by Maersk and layoffs were in the works. In some ways, that offered me great relief. I wasn't particularly high up, but I knew I would get several months of severance, which would give me some paid breathing room to start my next business.

However, that did not come to pass. My manager called me in and gave me the "good" news that they were planning on keeping me. It was flattering but bittersweet. In some ways I didn't have the courage to leave, so I wanted them to do it for me. They didn't, so I was stuck. That is, until I mulled it over for the week and decided it was selfish to keep a job I didn't want at the cost of a person who desperately needed it. Eventually, I resigned and decided to go see what I was made of. It felt good to be wanted but better to be free.

The status quo is quite the temptress in most cases. Change is scary, hard, and filled with uncertainties. Doing nothing is comfortable, safe, and has known returns (or a lack thereof). I like this quote from Neale Donald Walsch's *Conversation with God*: "Life begins at the end of your comfort zone."

My new but quickly failing company had little if any direction. I was making enough money to keep the lights on but doing nothing particularly inspiring. The staffing agencies I used to do contract work through would charge a company such as J.P. Morgan $80 per hour, pay me $60, and net $20. They never added any value and were basically doing nothing after matching a contractor for the needed work. I decided I could do that, but also add value. I recruited several of my colleagues and outlined the opportunity.

We formed a corporation, met three times a week, and focused on learning the most modern technology—the type of technology that would command the highest billing rates. We cut out the middleman and marketed directly to the companies in need. They saved money; we got the contracts, and they received better service and products. American Express was the first business to give us a shot, and they used a platform called Lotus Notes. We quickly became experts in it and essentially handled all their Lotus-based projects. Eventually, we also worked as the middleman when they needed manpower above and beyond what we could offer, so my small company was making it on both ends. We grew to twenty-five employees, all within the hallowed halls of this famous credit card and travel services company.

Things were moving along nicely at home as well. Later the same year, 1993, Larisa and I welcomed our first child, Stephanie. We outgrew our one-bedroom apartment the following year and moved to a quaint townhouse in North Brunswick, New Jersey. I was burning the candle at both ends, but my home and office lives were rewarding. I was living the hustle, and it was awesome. American Express led to Philip Morris, which led to the United Nations, which led back to J.P. Morgan as a direct customer this time.

Laptops had just reached the market, and that proved to be a game-changer. I'd work tirelessly late into the evening to build my new business. With it being in the financial district of Manhattan, I once again endured the ninety-minute each way commute from New Jersey that came along with it—on a comfortable commuter train this time. But I had a different mindset, one where I would maximize my abilities by using that commute to work, study, and learn. Learning more and more about programming, I began to further sharpen my skills.

We named the company Binary Tree, and in addition to selling application development services to businesses, we began to develop a line of software products. Almost overnight, we went from a little New York City-based business to an international player servicing huge corporations. By 1996, we began inking contracts with the likes of IBM, which acquired Lotus, providing them with a conversion product that would allow them to seamlessly onboard customers from competing systems to their email platform. It was amazing to think that a big company like IBM, with all its resources, couldn't do something that we could do. We were a needle in their haystack, but we provided them with a valuable product and service they couldn't provide on their own.

This helped me understand the value of being incredibly niche. We didn't do a fraction of what larger companies did, but what we did do, we did very well. That's really all it takes to succeed—do a few things better than just about everyone else out there. That was our secret sauce, and we followed it to a mathematical certainty. As our revenue continued to grow, collectively, our team decided to invest into our technology and future. It was amazing to watch, and while we were so young, we seemed to make calculated, thoughtful decisions that inevitably proved to support our evolution.

The successes began to come more often, but the grind never ended—day in and day out, commutes to the city, from the city, late nights, grueling project deadlines, payroll, benefits, 401(k), and needy customers who would drop you at a moment's notice. It wasn't easy to be an active and present husband and father, but I was fortunate Larisa understood the deep importance of our growth phase. Our parents would help on a regular basis as they were relatively close by. They were actively involved in our lives and in many ways were a great impetus for the continued development of Binary Tree. We couldn't have done it without them, and as immigrants, it was clear how much pride they took in my success.

Although my parents divorced at the time, they still maintained a polite, cordial relationship with each other and with my family. It was a pleasure to have them around, and we were all better for it. Once, my father visited my house and said, "Stevie, are you making $200,000 yet?"

I half laughed, knowing I was super close to that number. "Yeah, Dad, I sure am." I could see his glistening smile a mile away. You could see in his face the satisfaction of knowing that he had succeeded in capturing the American dream and passing it down for us to grab and run with. It seemed like life was aligning for us. We lived in a comfortable town-home in North Brunswick, in a development called Hidden Lake. It was a family-friendly community, and it was wonderful to socialize and get together with our family and neighbors over the weekends.

But for the most part, I was working. As much as I hoped for a work/life balance, I mostly focused on scaling Binary Tree. We were moving and moving fast. It felt like we had found something special, and we didn't want to lose our momentum. At the time, we didn't connect via video chat or even cell phones. Everything was done face to face. I would walk into large office buildings throughout the city, pause, and take a few deep breaths before pitching to an executive-filled room. I would become aware of my surroundings and awaken my senses to the moment. I would then close my eyes and visualize securing the project, winning the game, and walking off with a paying customer. It was a moment of truth, one that I would relish again and again. I knew we had what it took. I had come a long way since sitting in a small office waiting to get fired for introducing a bug into the *Reader's Digest* billing program.

It took some time, but life began to seem like a series of small finish lines, of goal setting and goal achieving. Nothing was out of mind, only momentarily out of sight. I could see myself, even feel myself, getting there. I don't think I fully realized it at the time, but we were steadily ahead of the curve. In many ways, my little company out of New York City was a cutting-edge tech company before such a thing really existed. That was one of our greatest assets. We were first in, pliable as they come,

Steven Pivnik - Built to Finish

and could pivot as quickly as we needed to. Nothing seemed to hold us back, and I was living on cloud nine at work.

At home was no different, but life wasn't always kind in even the best of circumstances. It was 1997, and Larisa was pregnant again. Baby Pivnik number two, due in a couple of months, was coming our way. We were excited to watch our family grow, but life had different plans for us. Larisa was at a routine doctor's visit one Saturday afternoon weeks before her due date when I got a call about some serious complications regarding the baby. Quickly, I put Stephanie in the car and sped off to Princeton, New Jersey. As luck would have it, I encountered bumper-to-bumper traffic and I had no cell phone to let Larisa know about the delay.

With cars at a near standstill, I began to fearlessly drive on the shoulder, caring little about being pulled over. After making illegal and unsafe good time for a few miles, a trucker saw me in his rearview mirror and pulled onto the shoulder to block any further progress. Truckers have no respect for anyone trying to pull off a move like this. Without serious thought, I drove up the grass embankment to pass the truck while horns blared from behind. Stephanie was fast asleep after we left our house and was oblivious to this drama. When I finally saw a police car, I pulled up and asked if I could get an escort. But he refused, indicating there was no one in immediate harm's way. At least he didn't mind me speeding off on the shoulder again.

I stayed focused on the road, eventually arriving at the office and running through the atrium and into the elevator, with my daughter in hand. What started as a wonderful dream ended as a total nightmare. When I arrived to see my hysterical wife, I learned that the doctor had just told her the fetus had no heartbeat and they were going to induce her to have a stillbirth. Despite how well things seemed to be going for us, I wasn't sure we would ever recover from this loss.

Although I was going a million miles per hour at work, this sudden news stopped me dead in my tracks, like hitting a brick wall at full speed. We had lost a child, and we had to mourn that tragic loss. It wasn't easy, but it was part of life. I learned a lesson that later endurance sports pounded into me even further: It is hard to predict ups and downs. You have to roll with the punches, welcoming in the good days but always remaining prepared, mentally and physically, for the difficult ones. Take time to mourn the losses, but remember that you have no choice but to carry on. We are who we are because of our experiences.

After losing a child via a stillbirth, our family faced the devastation and pain of what seemed like endless grief. It didn't pass quickly, and it didn't pass easily. I will never forget watching my wife go through labor, knowing that, at the end of what is supposed to be a joyous process, we would be left with a lifeless and breathless being. Watching Larisa's strength was the only thing that got me through that difficult time. She fought bravely through the pain and suffering of losing a child. Her bravery helped us through it. In typical fashion, I buried myself in work again, using my business as an escape from the pain and suffering of this experience.

We were lucky to have a living child, and we poured our love and attention into Stephanie to ease the pain. Time heals all wounds, but this was not a particularly easy recovery for anyone. Together, we found the collective courage to try again, and just a few years later we found ourselves pregnant with another child. It was a nerve-racking nine months, but along the way we experienced peace in knowing that we would get a wonderful second child.

And in the spring of 1999, along came another bundle of joy, Rochelle.

Key Takeaways

- One mistake does not define you. Don't let one mistake define others in your mind.

- Don't let the wrong motivations keep you stuck in the status quo.

- There is great value in being niche.

- You will face excruciatingly painful moments. Allow yourself to mourn, but remember to put one foot in front of the other and carry on.

SHOW UP, DON'T SLOW UP

IT WAS OFTEN CHALLENGING to maintain a vigorous training schedule while balancing good times with friends and family. Vacations were the hardest. Two memories come to mind here. One was in upstate New York when a group of my friends were going golfing in the morning. I asked if I could tag along in the car. "But you didn't bring clubs?" was their confused response. I asked them to drop me off ten miles from the cabin where we were staying so that I could run back and get in my training for the weekend. The other was in Arizona when most decided to go hot air ballooning one day. I took an Uber to a bike rental shop and went out for a hundred-mile bike ride in the heat instead.

I felt like I was growing my business in similar form and fashion. It was the roaring nineties, a time when computers and computer-related businesses were finding remarkable success. It was a time when nearly every company was updating networks, automating their business processes, and taking advantage of new technology. That boded well for a software-based technology company like ours. This was well before the internet became the main communication medium, so companies were still using disc drives and CDs to install software onto their computers. Burning new CDs day after day with our software on them to fulfill new orders was a ton of fun.

Our company had really found a niche: nothing sexy but nonetheless necessary and useful. At the time, most companies were using a variety of solutions to provide email and calendar functionality to their employees. It was hardly centralized like it is today. Each department in a large company would have their own email and calendar platform. When they realized the need to centralize their email and calendars, they had to figure out how to convert all of this data from one place to another. Nothing, and I mean nothing, was centralized and compatible with one another. It was nuts! That is where we came in. We developed software that could take all of this data and move it to a centralized enterprise-scale platform.

Enter Lotus, the large tech-based company that figured out how to offer scalable, secure, enterprise-grade email and calendar support to companies. As many of their customers decided to switch over, they needed our software to effectively migrate the data. We were doing pretty well and working with various companies throughout the country. But, our big break, the one that really put us on the map, came when we got a call from IBM, which had acquired Lotus. Initially, IBM figured it could quickly patch together software to import and centralize data onto its new system for customers. However, that wasn't its business model, and it didn't create a solution that worked all that well. So, IBM looked to the outside and found us. Rather than continuing to try to do this on its own, it scrapped its version of migration software and signed an agreement with Binary Tree to license our solution for two years.

That proved to be a true game changer. When IBM comes calling, you know you have made it. I went to Staples to make a color copy of the fat seven-figure check for posterity purposes, and the clerk laughed at me. "Sir, we're not allowed to make color copies of checks." I still have the black and white copy.

We went from a small company in downtown New York City to near worldwide notoriety overnight because our product's CDs were now being shipped in the same box with IBM's Lotus Notes. We were providing the conversion software to get a company's old email and calendar data to their new one. IBM agreed to allow us to brand our software, so everyone knew they were receiving a product from Binary Tree. This created a powerful snowball effect, as many large businesses began to reach out and ask if we could help them migrate their email and calendar data.

Because of these customers' size and the large amount of data they needed to migrate, it was practically essential that we not only provide the software but also the manpower to complete the job. Large customers across all industries and even governments chose Binary Tree for their mission critical email migration projects. It was a remarkable accomplishment and tremendous compliment to our abilities. We were signing six- and seven-figure contracts with multiple companies and growing rapidly. In some ways, it was hard to keep up. But in the same light, you couldn't say no to these opportunities. The answer was always yes, and we were scrappy enough to figure out how.

While saying yes led to continued growth, occasionally saying no would have led to significantly better profitability. We wanted to satisfy every customer's requirement as much as possible, so we rarely turned down a customization request. Had we said no more often, we could have kept our research and development costs down and increased the bottom line. But our approach kept us continuously ahead of the competition, so it made sense to continue.

Binary Tree began to hire like crazy, and with that came all the pains you'd expect with overnight growth. We had to build systems to scale, implementing better practices related to payroll, accounts receivable, accounts payable, HR functions, and corporate events. Culture became an important part of our daily conversations, and we did all we could to create an inviting culture that people wanted to be a part of. It was a work-hard, play-hard mentality, where we would put in fifty- to sixty-hour weeks but also find time to have meals as a company, go to nearby bars, or celebrate the holidays with elaborate parties.

We showed up every single day. There was no slow up for us. I was present in the business, every aspect of it. We had remarkable attention to detail, and I shot out of bed every single morning when my alarm clock went off at 6 a.m. There was simply no way I was going to take even one second of such a special experience for granted, and I tried to go above and beyond every single day in the office. I led by example and showed my team that I was going to be in the trenches with them working through challenges and building the business in a way that would lead to collaboration and a celebration of our individual and joint abilities.

I spent months on-site doing project work at customers like the United Nations, Phillip Morris, Merk, Sanofi Aventis, and Gartner, to name a few. I would take part in hundreds of sales presentations as the subject matter expert to the account executive leading the meeting, in addition to keeping my CEO card in my pocket for when it was needed. My favorite line was to leave a sales meeting saying, "Here is my card with my phone number on it. But I'll never hear from you because my team will ensure complete satisfaction." When my team heard me close with that, they knew they had to deliver.

However, there was one time when I did hear from them. We were running a project for a global company which required near around-the-clock support from us. The project was so complex that our head of technology got involved and was putting in his second twenty-four-hour shift when yet another large project hiccup occurred. He wasn't answering his phone when the client called, so I got a phone call at 2 a.m., which was 4 p.m. in Japan, letting me know that he was unresponsive. I had to call his wife in the middle of the night, just to make sure he was alright. She found him asleep at his home office desk. He snapped to and got right back to it.

I am proud to say that while growing Binary Tree, I held every single role in the business, from chief executive officer to chief financial officer to chief of running network cables through dropped ceiling tiles, and anything and everything in between. Your employees will respect you when you show them no task is beneath you, especially in the foundational days/years of a company.

We were always overworked and understaffed, so that called for an all-hands-on-deck mentality and a next-person-up attitude. A job always existed for an extra set of hands. It was a great feeling, as I got to step out of my leadership role and go back to my early days of coding. We had to get the job done, even if that meant the boss rolled up his sleeves and coded in front of a computer until the early morning hours. No one loves your business like you do. If you aren't willing to sacrifice and do what it takes to succeed, then how can you expect that anyone else will?

Binary Tree was a business of positive energy with a great culture. A great deal of immediate assimilation occurred; employees would quickly get comfortable and do a wonderful job. But, if you didn't fit in, it would spit you out. We never tolerated negative energy and would terminate employees who chose not to maintain a positive attitude. When someone became an energy vampire, that also was not tolerated for too long. We did try to coach and improve this type of behavior, and you would be surprised how thankful folks were when we called them out and asked them to improve. Another trait that I greatly disliked was gossip mongering. We all know who the gossip mongers are. They start most conversations with, "Did you hear?"

This is analogous to your mind starting to creep in with negative thoughts during a critical time in an endurance event or adventure. Fighting those negative thoughts is as hard, if not harder, than fighting water cooler gossip at work. On more than one mountain and in more than one race, I had to ask why I was still doing this to myself. "Enough already! You have nothing more to prove." The mind, being the most powerful muscle in the body, can just as quickly erase that negativity and get you back into the necessary rhythm and headspace needed to accomplish the task at hand.

More and more of today's workforce is looking for remote employment opportunities, but few have the experience of working outside of an office environment for an extended amount of time. Because we were pioneers in establishing a virtual workforce, we incorporated that aspect into our interviewing process to ensure we hired self-starters who would be motivated to work without the constant oversight of a boss. We did so because we learned the hard way that just because a candidate says they'll be fine working from home, they sometimes really are not. To ensure we stayed on track and aid in virtual assimilation, we created a quarterly new hire cohort across multiple departments. These virtual meetings allowed them to discuss their onboarding experience and share beneficial information with the group. We didn't take anyone for granted, but we also expected a lot from each and every team member.

At one point, the success of my own company almost embarrassed me. Rather than drive my brand-new Porsche, my dream car, to work, I purchased a beater—an old green Ford Bronco—for that job. I didn't want to be nicknamed "O.J.," so I got personalized plates that read "BIGSTEVE." This car didn't have any technology in it. No Bluetooth, no fancy screens, no nothing. I wasn't adhering to the new no-cell-phone policy just passed in New Jersey. I didn't have a wireless headset on either. Boy was it embarrassing to hear a police car pull behind me and bellow out, "Pull over, Big Steve," over their horn. I've saved those plates too and keep them with the copy of the IBM check.

Since writing about the past gives one the power of hindsight, I can say that I was probably wrong in how I felt about my success. While I was definitely proud, maybe I should have worn it on my sleeve a bit more often. I'm not saying being humble is inappropriate—not at all. But in most cases, it is OK to show that you are the boss and that you are successful, and therefore you can drive a nice car or wear a fancy watch. When I shared the Bronco purchase with a close executive of my company, his response put it all in better perspective. He said, "I'd rather work for a company whose owner drives a Porsche than a Bronco." I took that to heart. There was no returning the Bronco though.

Everything about my life seemed to improve. We moved to a bigger home, took more upscale vacations, and had several more extravagant experiences. It wasn't a rich and famous lifestyle, but we were definitely doing pretty well. I was doing a lot of personal work too, reading as much as I could and learning more and more about my industry and growing a business. I always felt like that offered me the greatest advantage to keep evolving and building something that could last.

While my business was experiencing significant success and growth, family life was humming along. We enjoyed our time with friends and loved a good night of food and adult beverages. Both of my parents were still alive and kicking but not without their challenges.

They didn't quite understand what I did, but they recognized that I did it well and were proud of my accomplishments. They were a unique generation and knew nearly nothing about computers. I had a hard enough time explaining data conversion to business professionals, so it wasn't easy at all to explain it to two immigrants without the faintest idea about technology. They just knew their son was the proud owner of a business and was self-employed. Nothing more and nothing less, but they could tell I was doing pretty well for myself.

The late '90s proved to be a special time for me and my business. The homerun with IBM resonated in my mind for a very long time. Just like with any dopamine hit, the mind and body craves the next one, and I knew in my bones that as long as we would continue to show up and never slow up there was another large at-bat around the corner.

I never stopped pounding the pavement, especially because we knew other companies were offering similar products and services. We had to constantly prove to all potential new customers that we were the best option and could outwork and outdeliver the competition. We didn't always have a plan or a well-conceptualized answer. But what we did do, every single day, was show up. I was fortunate to have assembled a team that truly bought in and cared deeply about our brand, our products, and customer satisfaction. As the bigger projects came rolling in, our dedication to showing up allowed us to succeed.

This was such a pivotal time and slowing up could have set us back a great deal. If you're staying the same, and your competition is improving, you're actually going backwards. You won't have a chance, and it is likely you'll get left behind. You never know when opportunity will knock, but you must be ready with your foot on the gas when it does. Motivational speaker Andy Albright said, "Showing up is important and it is a big part of becoming successful." I learned that early on in the life of my business. In many ways, you win the battle when you just get out of bed and show up. The rest is the rest. The work will come. Success will follow. All you have to do is show up and be ready for the next amazing opportunity that comes your way.

Key Takeaways

- Be present, daily.
- Monitor the pulse of your team to keep the positive culture rooted in work ethic you need for success.
- Never stop pounding the pavement. If you're not moving forward, you're going backward.

CRAVE THE RUSH

I AM ALWAYS PSYCHED to start any mountaineering adventure, but the rush leading up to my Aconcagua expedition takes the cake. Second in height of the seven summits only to Mount Everest, this majestic peak sits over 23,000 feet above sea level in the South American Andes Mountain range outside of Mendoza, Argentina. I was proud to be part of a strong team that included a retired US Marine, a forest firefighter, and other avid and capable climbers.

It took a few days to get to base camp, at 14,300 feet. After acclimatizing and ascending higher, a highly experienced climber in our group was stricken with high-altitude pulmonary edema (HAPE), a life-threatening form of altitude sickness. He was helicoptered down to sea level, which is the only remedy. As we said our tear-filled goodbyes, a wave of uncertainty enveloped me about the fate of the rest of us.

Speaking of waves, Binary Tree rode an unbelievable wave, one that was rapidly swelling and getting bigger and bigger right before our very eyes. The technology market was exploding and the dot-com era was in full swing. Our work with IBM snowballed into other contracts and opportunities with other large businesses across the country. Enjoying the influx, we were also working extremely hard, just trying to stay ahead of the game. In September 1999, a company approached us, interested in acquiring Binary Tree. Initially, it seemed like an exciting opportunity.

The company was already public and looking to acquire a similar company in the tech space. In many ways, this was a modern-day special purpose acquisition company (SPAC), before SPACs even existed. The business was intent on acquiring a company and taking on its name and business. It would have been a huge deal for us, tens of millions of dollars on paper. But as we entered due diligence, something wasn't quite adding up. In fact, I had a really bad feeling about the reverse merger the company was proposing. Even though the dollars were massive on paper, something didn't seem quite real to me. Getting deeper and deeper into the negotiations, I became more and more skeptical and hesitant. In the eleventh hour, right before we finalized the deal, I pulled the plug on it and took it to pasture.

Had we gone through with it, I would have given up 100 percent equity and control of Binary Tree, and it just wasn't the right call. I wasn't about to let my baby get thrown out with the bathwater for paper riches. That was somewhat disappointing since we had come so close to an exit. But as one door closes, another opens. About that time, a new startup, an application service provider called netASPx, which was essentially an early software as a service company (SaaS), approached us to acquire the professional service side of our business. This was a totally different deal, a real one, with real dollars, and had a totally different feel.

It was a hard negotiation, and I regularly pushed back, refusing to accept offer after offer. I ended up flying down to their headquarters in

Herndon, Virginia, to meet face-to-face with the CEO. Just like in the movies, on one fateful evening, with the sun setting over the fall foliage, the CEO pulled out a napkin and wrote a large number on it. Smiling, he said, "Is this enough?" Perhaps I just wanted to get the deal, or maybe it actually was enough. Either way, I told him I would take the deal back to my partners at the time and let him know. The new deal had a cash component and an earnout component, so I would make some good money on the sale and remain employed with the new company with upside potential if my division financially performed as forecasted.

Between Thanksgiving and Christmas, we hammered out the details. The plan was for me and my team on the professional services side to join netASPx as they purchased only this portion of our company. I was happy. My partners were happy. This was the next step in our evolution and a lucrative deal that would usher in a totally new layout of Binary Tree. We had to share the news with our staff. No one was getting fired, but we were effectively splitting our company into two separate parts, one team remaining at Binary Tree and another team coming with me to netASPx.

I sent two emails to the staff. One email was directed to the people staying, the other was directed to the people going. We sent staff members to two separate locations for two separate meetings, and the now separate leadership teams broke the news. All in all, it was exciting news, and everyone took it in stride. There were no hard feelings as this was based on job descriptions, not one team being better than the other.

I became a millionaire overnight. This was somewhat euphoric for me and one of the largest wins in my young career. I still remember, to this day, meeting with my new broker at Merrill Lynch. He said, "Steven, how aggressive do you want to be with this? It is a lot of money, but on a scale from one to ten, how aggressive?" The stock market was out of control, and totally oblivious to the bubble we were in. I said, "Thirteen! That's how aggressive I want to be. You've got to kill this for me." Sadly, my distribution of wealth would be short-lived. My broker killed it all right; he killed a hefty chunk of every dollar I invested with him. I was craving the rush, and this time, it backfired.

Even so, I wasn't struggling. With a new position at netASPx, I was about to embark on my MBA in a box, taking a position of leadership and wearing an entirely new hat. I came to netASPx as the Director of Consulting Services and was later promoted to Vice President of Customer Implementations. It was amazing to work alongside my colleagues who had just raised more than $75 million for the company from a very reputable private equity firm. Talk about a stark contrast from my boot-strapped former company struggling to make payroll.

At Binary Tree, I was tasked with waking up every single day and just hustling, totally working my ass off. Now, I was in a corporate setting with real objectives and financial deliverables. I could no longer operate on gut and instinct. I had shareholders to whom I had to answer. When I arrived at netASPx, my focus shifted to working with seasoned executives creating sales strategies and marketing plans and monitoring staff utilization levels, average billing rates, and a whole bunch of other margin-based objectives to ensure we were growing and profitable. My new role involved significant structure, and, along with my team, I had to adjust.

I attended real board meetings, not the fly-by-night get-togethers at the neighborhood bar like we'd had at Binary Tree. We would review financials, profitability, and address a myriad of hard questions. I was tasked with conducting formal assessments, salary reviews, and the necessary evil performance-improvement plans. We had to figure out who we would hire, who we would fire, and who we would work to develop.

Then, the dot-com collapse had arrived. In mid-2000, the bottom really fell out of the market, and our business suffered like many others. We were forced to start laying off a lot of staff. NetASPx had just acquired six other companies, in addition to Binary Tree, and most of them reported to me through various levels of middle management. It felt horrible to tell hundreds of people they no longer had jobs. But, unfortunately, that is what I had signed up for.

Just like when we had split our staff in two at Binary Tree to deliver the acquisition news, we would send out calendar invites with two con-ference call-in numbers. Depending on which call each employee joined, they were either told about the unfortunate reduction in staff that was occurring or told they were part of the reduction and no longer had a job.

It was gut-wrenching to go from riding the wave and flying high a few months before to what became a pretty challenging situation. Simultaneous to my experience at netASPx, Binary Tree was also coming on tough times. When I left, I put a new CEO in place to manage the day-to-day business. It shocked me to learn that Binary Tree was suffering, and my baby, that I had built from the ground up, was teetering on total catastrophe. I felt stuck. On one hand, I had committed to netASPx and the new business. I wanted it to succeed. But on the other, Binary Tree needed me.

Thankfully, timing was the answer. NetASPx was laying people off, but it was contractually obligated to pay me a hefty salary. Recognizing Binary Tree needed me, I offered to forego my salary and leave the com-pany. NetASPx agreed to let me go, and I returned to Binary Tree in hopes of whipping it back into shape. It was sobering to return to my ailing company. I hadn't done a great job of keeping tabs on the finan-cials, mostly since I was entrenched in my role at netASPx. If you own a company or a substantial portion of one, you owe it to yourself to receive and review monthly financial statements—or at the very least quarterly, preferably prepared by a reputable accounting firm that you personally have hired.

It was August 2001, and Binary Tree was on life support. When I returned, I took a step back and realized it wouldn't make sense to just oust the current, now second CEO since my departure, and take over. Besides, I had a little bit of hope that with my assistance, he would get us through the tough times.

I returned to Binary Tree as an account executive (i.e., a door-to-door salesman), in many ways reverting back to my roots. I believed I could nurse my baby back to health by being the best salesman I could possibly be. Generating business would be the key to our success and revitalization. I had a close personal relationship with the CEO and completely trusted him. That gave me peace, as I was burned out of management and needed a break after netASPx. I quickly decided to keep my head in the sand, dial for dollars, and just focus on generating business and nothing more. I wasn't asking for financial statements. I didn't care who was measuring what. That was, unfortunately, the recipe for yet another problem.

At that same time, the United States and the world would be encountering a major problem of their own. Being in sales, during my daily cold-calling activity in late August 2001, I had scheduled a meeting on the ninety-eighth floor of the World Trade Center. I called to confirm my appointment by leaving a voicemail on September 10. On September 11, my train from New Jersey entered Penn Station in Manhattan and I was about to get on the subway to head downtown for my 8:30 a.m. meeting. Remembering that my phone call was never returned, and the meeting was not confirmed, I headed to our midtown office instead. The rest is sad history.

World issues led to more business ones. The following month, our preferred bank and primary lender surprised me with a phone call. Since I personally guaranteed our line of credit, they let me know that they hadn't received interest payments for our credit line for nearly three months. I was shocked and couldn't believe my second CEO—a guy I trusted—had let me down as well. Binary Tree had an office in Minnesota, where he was working, so I boarded the next flight out to confront him. As I learned more details, I realized I had no choice but to fire him, which I did.

I had to stop dialing for dollars and take on a leadership position again. Over the next few days, I would interview every one of the current staff to determine if they should remain at their job or move on. This ridiculous ambivalence started from above but festered throughout the entire organization. This wasn't the culture we built. After three days on site and a deep dive into interviews with each staff member, I leaned out our team to just enough people to get the job done. Rightsizing to a staff of only about a dozen was the first step in keeping the ship afloat.

Now knee-deep in debt, we had to figure out our next steps. I started by calling every single one of our vendors to explain our dilemma. I renegotiated the debt, explaining that we could either file for bankruptcy, voiding their balance with us completely, or they could accept a reduced payment. I negotiated pennies on the dollar, and slowly but surely, we began to climb out of the terrible hole our former leadership team had dug, including making right on two missed payrolls. It took a while, but every present and past employee who was asked to take one for the team got the money they were rightfully owed.

Leaving for netASPx was a difficult decision, but I am glad I did it. It wasn't an easy two years there, but it was very educational and rewarding in many respects. In some ways, the experience gave me a much greater appreciation for what I had at Binary Tree. I realized how hard it was to work in a traditional corporate structure—always on the road, traveling from city to city and office to office, managing hundreds of people. This was not easy stuff in the least. Larisa and I now had two young children and things were quite busy on the home front. In addition to our Minnesota office, we also had our office in Manhattan and clients around the country, so it seemed like I was living out of a suitcase again. We had crazy hours, different time zones, and a whole bevy of travel.

Some of my largest takeaways from this larger company experience included their processes related to reporting, measurements, KPIs, and accountability. Being scrutinized by a large private equity investor required that we carefully assess and look at every financial detail within. We then had to remain disciplined and stay on top of our numbers to try and avoid surprises. These were the type of practices I instilled in Binary Tree when I returned.

My wife was also working, as an accountant. We had a live-in nanny because we both were constantly working. However, we spent our weekends together as a family, focusing on the kids' activities, hanging out with friends and family, and getting out and about. Part of the benefit of returning to Binary Tree was a return to a much more simple and free life. I could, for the most part, make my own schedule and spend time with my family and friends, albeit around my still prioritized work life. Sure, the travel was fun, but it took a lot out of me. The endless trade shows, wining and dining, and amazing events made up part of the hype of the post-dot-com economic resurgence. That was part of the rush. But a return to my roots was also extremely meaningful and purposeful.

One of many memorable moments with Stephanie occurred during this time. We had gone for a walk to our development's town center. We got a couple of sodas and some chips, heading in the direction of the playground. We plopped down on an inclined grassy field to enjoy the sun and our snacks. The weather was clear. We enjoyed the sun on our skin, a slight breeze in the air—a perfect father-daughter outing. "Dad, this is the best time ever!" are words that I will never forget hearing. Many people think that extravagant vacations are needed to create great memories. In one sentence, Stephanie negated that entire premise.

I haven't always heeded the lesson Stephanie taught me. I craved the rush so bad that sometimes I signed up for some crazy events that also took me away from home. At the top of the list was a triathlon called Escape from Alcatraz. The night before the race Larisa and I took an excursion to visit this legendary penitentiary. We were being rocked pretty bad in the tour boat crossing the San Francisco Bay, and I knew exactly what she was going to say. Sure enough, she said, "How the hell are you going to swim in this tomorrow?"

The next morning, all the competitors boarded a large ferry boat which took us out to Alcatraz Island. It anchored right off the shore of "The Rock" and the gun went off, our signal to jump off the boat into the fifty-two-degree water five at a time and swim the one and a half miles towards the beach of the St. Francis Yacht Club in a very strong current. While there were hundreds of other swimmers around me, it was hard to tell due to the enormous swells. After the swim it was off to the grueling eighteen-mile bike course through this incredibly hilly city. As if my legs weren't burning enough, all I needed to complete this race and finish was a very demanding eight-mile run through the Golden Gate National Recreational Area.

I was disappointed with my finishing time of four hours and thirty-three minutes, but this is one event I probably won't be repeating to obtain a new personal record. I say this for a few reasons. In some cases, it's totally OK to be one and done. Many people feel that way after a triathlon. They wear that finisher medal with pride, as they should, and don't need a repeat performance. That's how I feel about Escape from Alcatraz. I'm proud that I tried it and finished it and will relish in the sense of accomplishment. If I didn't finish however, there is a great chance that I would be back to address unfinished business at this very unique and bucket list race venue.

This concept applies to business as well. If you're not happy with the outcome of an initiative, you should learn from it and move on. Sometimes doubling down is the right thing to do, and other times it can be an example of throwing good money after bad. Make the decision wisely.

It is a strange dynamic when you are constantly running, closing deals, and living in the air. Each one of these experiences proved to be a little dopamine pop, riding the rush. At first, while at netASPx, I craved the ability to lead as well as the respect that goes along with it. That definitely felt good. Returning to Binary Tree, my rush was turning calls into dollars and signing up new business. Those were my so-called wins. In any case, I needed something to keep me going; a lit fire under my ass. The beauty of the business rush. I could fulfill it in so many ways. I didn't want it to come to an end.

This was a true time of transition and a valuable one at that. I experienced so many lessons and takeaways as I chased the rush of success. It seemed to me that, at least for my transition to netASPx and then back to Binary Tree, timing was everything. NetASPx was doing a lot of remarkable things in the tech world, but it was just a little too early. There's no such thing as a coincidence, and everything worked out as planned. It would be easy to have looked at the move to netASPx as a mistake, but it gave me the exciting opportunity to learn about leadership, management, and professional financial and corporate governance. I took these skills and returned to Binary Tree with a newfound love and respect for my business and how to properly run it and be a steward for its success.

My biggest mistake? My inexperience in oversight while I was away, blindly trusting one CEO and then another, and believing in the notion that key executives would simply do the right thing. Fool me once shame on you, fool me twice shame on me. Perhaps that is why, even now, I hesitate to say that aggressively chasing the rush is always the best move. It must be tempered and not the tunnel focus of your attention. The rush must be replenished, again and again, and it often feels like we are constantly looking for the next best thing. As my story unfolds, you will see how I replaced the rush of business with that of climbing mountains, running marathons and ultramarathons, and competing in triathlons. But one thing I can tell you, unequivocally, is that the rush can motivate you or it can sink you. The choice is yours and yours alone.

There is one rush that went from up to down to impactful. On Mount Aconcagua, after the evacuation of our teammate, we continued to ascend, hoping for a summit bid which came many days later. By then it was down to our lead guide, the Marine, the forest firefighter, and me. I was beyond honored to make it to the top with this distinguished group.

As if we weren't exhausted enough, the Marine wanted to give tribute to his fellow soldiers. He shared with me the statistic that on average, twenty-two veterans a day commit suicide. So that is the number of pushups he asked me to join him in. Being forever grateful for the men and women that protect the freedom my family and I enjoy, I immediately obliged.

Key Takeaways

- Detours in life will happen. Just make sure you learn from them and bring the new skills you learned along the way with you when you're back on your path.

- Entrepreneurs crave the rush—be careful not to chase the rush just for the adrenaline high.

- Find multiple ways to have the rush in your life so that you can choose the right rush at the right time.

- Honor the men and women who protect your freedoms at every chance you get.

CELEBRATE THE
SMALL THINGS

WHEN I FIRST EMBARKED on my triathlon journey, I created a customized frame to hang in my home gym for motivation. It consisted of three classic shots of the IRONMAN World Championship in Kona, Hawaii. One was of the swim in Kalua Bay taken by an underwater diver, showing the flowing motion of the swimmers above. The second was of a dozen athletes, spaced out, grinding it out on the hilly bike course of the Queen Ka'ahumanu Highway, commonly called the Queen K Highway. In the third, exhausted runners silhouetted against the sunset completing the final leg of this grueling test of endurance and perseverance.

Looking at this collection almost daily was a continuous reminder of how hard yet simple this crazy hobby is. Swim effortlessly, bike continuously, and run intentionally. Do these things consecutively, and you will claim your prize.

My collection of photographs also brings to mind this Vincent van Gogh quote I love: "Great things are done by a series of small things brought together." This describes his painting style, often recognized as a great deal of dramatic, bold brushstrokes that form a remarkable, beautiful masterpiece. How an artist uses a series of calculated but immaculate movements of their chosen tool has always fascinated me. While I am far from a renowned artist, I knew I had some substantial work to do to get my masterpiece, Binary Tree, back in good order.

Eventually, I took back control of Binary Tree. It wasn't my goal, but it was the best thing for the health and future success of the business. I found it funny to look around my own company and see so many new faces. I had to ask each employee what they did, who hired them, and what they liked and didn't like about working there. These meetings and the knowledge I obtained led to some tough decisions. After retaining only the bare essential staff and letting go of a good number of employees, we were left with only a skeleton crew that we needed to keep the lights on.

I appreciated every team member who chose to stay on and live up to their job responsibilities. Some that we asked to stay still left. I respected those decisions as well because I knew their hearts wouldn't be in it. Skill sets are important, but passion fuels real performance. The ones who stayed were happy to have me back, recognizing positive change was coming. The team felt like some adult supervision finally existed again, and I promised each of the remaining staffers I would take care of them, never miss a payroll, and would remain dedicated to bringing the glory days back to Binary Tree. Easier said than done, though.

We were still drowning in debt—so much so that our primary lender could have easily foreclosed on the company's line of credit, which was fully drawn at the time and which I had personally guaranteed; I had put my home up as collateral. That was a scary moment, a sink or swim time. The bank showed some mercy, and I promised I would make good on every penny I owed. To that end, I promised that I would meet with the bank's workout team every month for continuous reviews. This is not a group you ever want to meet with at a bank. Their sole goal is to get the bank's money bank, either through repayment or through foreclosure.

I wanted to show up in a big way, so I traveled to Manhattan monthly and presented myself in a suit and tie. This meant a lot to me, and I think it meant a lot to the bank. I don't think most of their debtors came into the city to give them financial updates in person. But the bank personnel were showing such grace to me and my company, and I wanted them to feel comfortable as well. I spent our hourly monthly meeting communicating company updates and financial forecasts and discussing the payback schedule. We did not miss a single commitment I made to them.

Month after month, we chipped away at the debt and paid back every penny, plus interest, that we owed. It wasn't easy, but I celebrated the opportunity to turn things around. My transparency with the bank, and nearly everyone else involved in my business, mattered a great deal. It was a great comeback story for us. But that wasn't the only problem we faced. In addition to the bank debt, we were fighting substantial healthcare debt. We were a self-insured company, meaning that we provided and covered most healthcare costs for our staff. This avoided hefty monthly insurance premiums, but we had to shell out some serious cash when people got sick.

About this same time, several team members became pregnant. Babies aren't cheap. Additionally, and tragically, a few team members received far less than pleasant diagnoses that resulted in expensive treatment. The insurance balance hit six figures, and I had to negotiate that down to a reasonable amount and pay it off over a five-month period. Month after month, we drew closer and closer to breaking even. The debt felt insurmountable, but just like an artist's painting, one broad stroke after another, we inched ever closer to financial health.

Once, to show goodwill, I even wrote the bank a personal six-figure check just to take a bite out of the debt. I didn't have to do it, but it felt like the right thing to do. If they couldn't trust me and offer me enough rope to be flexible, I would be out for the count. In my mind, it was the least that I could do.

We weren't just facing monetary challenges, though. Our relationship with IBM continued to be our most profitable contract. Lotus Notes was the de facto enterprise email platform, and hundreds of companies representing millions of end users turned to our software to migrate data when they deployed IBM's platform. But as they say, don't count a good man out. At about the same time, Microsoft began to make a massive push to rule the corporate email market, rolling out new and improved versions of Microsoft Outlook and Exchange. This was well before the cloud, and they finally figured out a way to offer up a scalable, reliable, and less virus-prone enterprise email and calendar platform.

Amazingly, we started to get calls from our customers asking if we could migrate them from Lotus to Microsoft. We fought the requests. We were loyal to IBM. The company had done so much for our business. However, those requests went from being infrequent to extremely regular. We didn't want to defect to the "Dark Empire," as IBM called it. But we couldn't lose the opportunity either. At work, we began to secretly develop software that would work with Outlook and Exchange. Slowly, rumors began to leak that Binary Tree was developing software to work with Microsoft. It became somewhat of an uncomfortable situation.

Around this time, we attended a large annual trade show, hosted by

IBM, called Lotusphere. At the end of it, our head of marketing attempted to register for the following year's show. The registrar wasn't very receptive to our application. "We're sorry, but we can't let you register for next year." It was clear they had received some marching orders from above, and I didn't want to rock the boat. Besides, the cat was clearly out of the bag. In response, I decided to set up a meeting with IBM brass. To this day, it was one of the most uneasy feelings I've ever experienced.

Nonetheless, I walked into the meeting with some of their executives in Westchester, New York, ready to spill the beans that we were developing for Microsoft. As I started in, a senior executive interrupted me. He was so gracious in his words. "Steven, I can tell you're nervous. But remember: Every single relationship has a beginning, a middle, and an end. Don't worry about it. We know it's not personal, and you've got to do what you've got to do." And with that, we were open for business with Microsoft.

Actually, for many years to follow, we had our cake and ate it too. Due to the strong reputation we developed in the IBM/Lotus market, companies that needed our original software continued to do business with us while we were building up our brand and capabilities with Microsoft.

I was still the chief cook and bottle washer at Binary Tree, but I refocused my efforts on helping the development of the new software. We were reengineering products and deep in the trenches. There were many late nights of coding and going on-site to customer projects with my team of experts behind the scenes to transform our software. I felt like I was back in my element, returning to the essence of our business. It was nonstop, and we were full speed ahead.

It was 2003, and with the new opportunity in clear view, I began to hire again and grow our staff. Because we'd paid back every penny to the bank, we were able to open a new credit line with a larger bank. Keeping our credit in good order and avoiding bankruptcy was yet another win for us. That small win offered us the opportunity to get money when we needed it the most.

As business grew domestically, we were also getting calls from various parts of Europe. England first, then France, then nearly every part of the EU. Companies in Australia and Asia followed suit. They all wanted our software, as they were experiencing technology trends similar to America's. Binary Tree started to hire staff abroad, and for the first time was becoming more of an international company. That, in many ways, was the cherry on top of our comeback. I loved to travel and now could go all over the world for business. What a great deal!

It was like IBM was the big shark in the ocean, and we were the little pilot fish just swimming by its side, strategically positioned to benefit from any scraps in its wake. Comparatively speaking, we didn't need much to survive. When Microsoft took over and became the big fish in the ocean, we took a similar pilot fish-like approach and swam next to them and did our job. More and more companies chose Microsoft's platform, and that created an amazing uptick in our business. We had Lotus Notes, and now we had Microsoft Exchange. In many ways, this was Binary Tree's most growth-oriented time.

Our migration and integration work exploded. We couldn't hire enough people to stay on top of everything. It was amazing to watch. Talk about a comeback story. Binary Tree was on its knees choking for air when I returned, and just a few years later we were back in top form. For the first time in a long time, I felt a sense of peace. It seemed like everything was going to be just fine.

Things at home were par for the course, with the girls finding themselves, growing, learning, and falling in love with dance. If I wasn't working, I was driving the kids to and from dance practice or competition. Thankfully, laptops and cell phones had become commonplace, so I did plenty of work while waiting on them to finish practice at a local studio. Things were going my way, and I knew we were doing good work.

It was quite the honor when we were chosen to be on the Inc. 500 list, which represented the 500 fastest growing companies in America. We celebrated that recognition and later made the new and expanded Inc. 5000 list for seven years in a row, which showed our remarkable growth and success. Each passing year of recognition seemed to feel better than the previous one.

I like collecting awards. Medals from the races I compete in are great symbols of personal accomplishments, but company awards meant even more to me. My pride was more about the recognition of the success of our now international team. In many ways, it was an opportunity for me and my team to pause and celebrate where we had come from and where we were headed. The companywide email I would send out announcing any new award read like an Oscars acceptance speech, but the entire cast—not me—was the star. I thanked everyone for their contribution toward the recognition. Binary Tree had landed, and we were doing the right thing to continue its success and growth.

Now, we needed to organize Binary Tree in a way that made sense. We had an ever-increasing number of contracts and clients, and each team had to do its job and stay focused on the target. I also made sure the business was very transparent. We had an all-hands-on-deck mentality, but we were organized in a way where each team and member knew which deck they were standing on. The engineers would code; the consultants would work directly with the clients; customer support would deal with helping customers after the consultants moved on to the next project, and so on.

The efficiencies of scale were quickly taking over, and it was wonderful to see team members excel in their respective roles.

We were methodical and strategic, and we focused on our goals. It was a pleasure to watch, and I loved chipping in anywhere and everywhere that was needed. A great energy infused our culture, and I loved going to work each day. Looking back, it was really about doing the small things in the right way and then, when we did, celebrating our success. It was about making incremental improvements to ensure that we built enough steam to power the high-performing engine. The relationship with Microsoft continued to improve. I remember roaming their sprawling campus in Redmond, Washington, meeting with top executives, and thinking, *Wow! So this is the house that Bill (Gates) built?*

That was a powerful moment in my life and in the life of Binary Tree. I smiled ear to ear and paused to celebrate such a tremendous moment in my professional life. But that was just the product of our hard work. I never took one team member for granted; I always valued and appreciated what they brought to the table. My Ukrainian origins inspired me to celebrate nearly everything. Hell, Ukrainians would celebrate the fact that it is Friday. It doesn't take much to excite us.

I tried to apply that same energy and attitude to work. It should be fun. We should pause and celebrate all of our accomplishments. If we couldn't find a big reason to celebrate, we would come up with one. To ensure our team felt supported and valued, we implemented company matching to our 401(k) plan, enhanced our bonus program, and offered several other attractive benefits, including a stock option plan to employees. This kept our current team happy, and we began to attract the best and brightest in the industry. These small, incremental steps fueled the engine, and everyone was firing on all cylinders.

Most of these team members were used to being taken for granted, either in the dark days of Binary Tree or through other employers. They were rarely celebrated, even when they hit a home run. Not at my company. Though we grew to over a hundred employees, we were still considered a relatively small company by industry standards, but we were on the map and a force. I wanted to share that information with my team. I made a habit of *over*communicating and showing tremendous appreciation for even the smallest of wins.

These wins add up and eventually become the conduit for your growth and success. In and out of the boardroom, business leaders often take small victories for granted. That is a shame because every win, even the seemingly small ones, should be celebrated. It is easy to only focus on the home runs, but the singles, especially if there are enough of them, can win you the game as well.

Key Takeaways

- Never underestimate the power of the personal touch to demonstrate your commitment.
- Embrace your inner Ukrainian and celebrate the small victories.

PUTTING IN
THE WORK

RUNNING IN PERFECT WEATHER IS EASY. Biking without significant elevation gain is not that challenging. Open water swimming without two-to-four-foot swells will keep your lunch down. There is no substitute for work. Mostly hard work. It's not always easy to climb out of bed when the alarm goes off at 5 a.m. I'd be lying if I said that I beat my urge to get back under the covers all of the time, but I'm thankful that the ratio is significantly in my favor. Building endurance and strength for the marathon of life, business, and sport is far from easy, but few things worth doing in life are.

Recently, during a heavy snowstorm in New York, I had to get in a five-mile run, but was I sick and tired of the treadmill. I bundled up in a weatherproof top and hit the Central Park reservoir loop to the astonished eyes of tourists who were out for a snow-filled Manhattan morning stroll. "Now that's hardcore," is all that I remember hearing through the fog of the bone-chilling, feet-numbing cold I was experiencing. It was almost identical to a guys' trip I'd taken to the Catskills a few years back where a winter wonderland materialized and, to everyone's amazement, I emerged from my bedroom in my running gear and let my pals know I would be back in a couple of hours because I needed to get my run in.

The work isn't easy. If it were, everyone would do it. We would wake up earlier than anyone else and stay up later than the competition. In some ways, I am thankful everyone didn't have the same attitude my team and I had. If that were the case, it would have been even harder to get ahead and build something that lasted. You see, Binary Tree worked. We avoided near disaster in the earlier 2000s to build something that would last. As we passed 2005, 2006, and 2007, our team recognized not just tremendous growth but remarkable outcomes. After a series of pivots and adjustments, we were firing on all cylinders and we could feel it—the culture, the hard work, the dedication to the bottom line, and the impressive results we achieved.

I would always be the first one in and the last one out, meaning that no one in my company or my competition would outwork me. My personal approach manifested itself in our partnering approach with the big boys. That foundational attitude was perhaps a reason why we forged such a strong relationship with IBM and then again with Microsoft. They saw the hard work and wanted a company like Binary Tree by their side. Whether we were at a trade show with Microsoft or creating a deliverable for them, they would recognize our work ethic and ability to deliver quality solutions.

That went a long way toward establishing and cementing a lasting relationship with this amazing company that was quickly becoming the leader in the enterprise email market. We went above and beyond as a team and built relationships that would span well beyond our software. We grew within the ranks of the Microsoft Business Partner ecosystem and eventually won the coveted Partner of the Year Award. We seemed to have lucked into yet another remarkable partnership. Maybe it wasn't luck. As famed film producer Samuel Goldwyn put it, "The harder I work, the luckier I get." Our reputation and expertise in the email migration business was a huge sell for the industry, and it made us a very attractive business. Now, we just had a different guiding light.

Nonstop trade shows and smaller road shows happened a lot during this time, which created a kind of wild west environment in the industry. Microsoft went right after IBM, surgically picking off IBM's vast email market share in the corporate space. As the tides turned, there was a substantial shift from IBM's Lotus Notes to Microsoft Exchange and later their cloud version, Office 365, now known as Microsoft 365, as the preferred enterprise email platform. Trade show after trade show, we were right by Microsoft's side, playing on their reputation but also sponsoring their events, breakout sessions, and parties to attract more customers. While Microsoft was the 800-pound gorilla in our industry, we were also fortunate to serve many other large companies around the world. If you threw a dart at a list of the world's largest companies, you were 95 percent guaranteed to hit a Binary Tree customer.

Traditionally, Microsoft would work with multiple partner companies to offer the similar solutions, so we were still competing against other migration solution providers. We would share the stage, and I would be front and center, selling to the audience and showing them why Binary Tree's products were the only choice. We were in the midst of an intense competition that made us work harder and harder. Little room for error existed, and we were OK with that. We were built for this type of game, mostly because we were the best solution, and we knew it. Hell, our competition knew it.

We weren't cocky. Rather, we truly believed in what we offered, and we delivered accordingly. Great software wasn't enough to get the job done. We implemented an incredible professional services and customer support program, helping companies execute these complex projects with our staff and also troubleshooting any issues they encountered on their projects. It was imperative to ensure every single project went off without a hitch. We wanted our clients to go back to Microsoft and sing our praises. How else could we maintain the relationship?

Even though things were going quite well with Microsoft, we didn't stop innovating. Binary Tree kept its ear to the ground to understand exactly what was happening in the industry, always trying to be at the forefront of changing technology. We knew our competition, the key players, and industry needs. There was no mystery involved. This wasn't guesswork. It was methodical. Surgical. Precise. So much so that when Google decided to throw their hat into the ring, we were ready.

Google, with its Gmail product, was a major player in consumer email. The company decided to create a similar enterprise platform and offer it to the business industry. If Google was going to get enterprise email market share, we wanted to benefit from the migration effort that would be required. While it took us some effort to figure out who the relevant executives were, we eventually found a name and I took the next flight out to California to meet with them. It proved an interesting time for us, working with a quickly fading IBM, a monster in Microsoft, and now this new-to-market behemoth, Google. We started working with Google, and they wrote us a fat check to develop migration software, but our relationship didn't last long.

While IBM took our work with Microsoft in stride, Microsoft didn't offer similar sentiments in relation to our work with Google. Executives politely told us that it wasn't cool to see their logo right next to Google's as a migration option on our website. We didn't have to read between the lines on this one as they made it clear that something had to change. Almost overnight, we killed our relationship with Google, took them off our website, and never worked with them again. In the end, it was a great decision because Google's enterprise email endeavor never really materialized, and to this day they carry a very small market share.

This was a very expensive lesson learned for Google. They just assumed they could carry over their dominance in the consumer email space to the large enterprise space. The opposite was true for Microsoft. Enterprise dominance didn't give them any success in markets like smart phones and music players. Expansion into new markets is always a very tempting drug, if these industry behemoths have challenges, then us scrappy entrepreneurs need to learn from their mistakes. Staying in your lane is sometimes the best strategy.

At Binary Tree, we continued to enjoy a work hard, play hard mentality. That attitude created a wonderful culture, and although we were a first in, last out kind of business, we didn't waste a lot of time sweating the small things. Together, we became virtual before virtual was cool, offering our staff the opportunity to work from home. That shifted our conversation and hiring perspective to hire the best and the brightest, not necessarily anchored to any specific geography, unlike many other companies. We could cherry-pick talent from all across the world and equip them with the tools that would allow them to get the job done from the West Coast, Midwest, or even internationally. Slowly, but surely, our staff lived in fifteen states and twelve countries. It was a remarkable example of our diversity, which proved to be one of our greatest strengths.

Workplace diversity has become an important issue, and I am proud that we recognized the value in hiring people from different backgrounds early on and prioritized that when staffing our company. When the diversity crisis came to a head, we were one of the few companies around that didn't have to change a single thing in our hiring practices.

Our hiring philosophy was very straightforward. Hire the best person possible for the job. Period. The needed skillset and cultural fit were evenly weighted for all candidates. If one has a learning mindset, they will actually attempt to get a better relationship with someone who is different from them and learn from the camaraderie that develops.

Since we were located all around the world, we implemented an annual holiday party that drew us all together in one place. Whether it was Las Vegas, New Orleans, Florida, or some other exciting location, we blew it out. Binary Tree would fly in each team member and his or her significant other and put them up in a nice hotel. We'd enjoy an extravagant weekend together, cutting it up and celebrating what we'd built.

Year after year, we raised the stakes. One year, we featured a Britney Spears impersonator for entertainment, and the next it was a party at a nightclub with a Bill Gates impersonator—my favorite, for obvious reasons. I think he did a better job than I did coming out as Borat another year to announce and hand out awards to the staff, gray suit and chicken bag included. But throughout the years, one night stands out above the rest. That year, we planned to hold our annual get-together in Princeton, New Jersey. Prior to the weekend, my head of sales, who was organizing the event, asked if I would mind being roasted during the affair. A good sport, I was totally fine with it. It is part of my self-deprecating sense of humor, and I figured it would be fun for the staff to watch the old boss get hammered by some comedian.

Well, to my surprise, that random person ended up being none other than Gilbert Gottfried. The funniest part of it? I assumed that he was an impersonator. He started off with "*Pivnik?* What type of name is *Pivnik?* That sounds like a venereal disease! Don't go near him, he has PIVNIK!" And the roast continued. *This guy is good*, I thought. *Just like the real thing.* Well, that's because he was the real Double G himself! You'd recognize his voice a mile away over the sound of a train coming.

At first, it was exciting and fun to have these blowout parties, knowing we would get together, celebrate our annual success, and just decompress. But on this night with Gottfried, these celebrations would come to bite me in the ass. He made sure of it. The roast was one for the ages, and Gottfried didn't pull any punches. He was raunchy, kind of mean, and ripped me to shreds. It was classic and tons of fun. One of my team members was so offended by the comedian's content, however, that he left the room and was followed by a supportive colleague. I don't blame them. I've got the routine saved on video, but rarely show it. Gottfried would eventually pass away, far too soon. I remember him as a legend and feel honored that he drove through a blizzard from Manhattan to Princeton to stick to his commitment.

This was a very valuable lesson learned and one that in today's environment would have cost us dearly. Pushing the envelope is one thing, but going overboard needs to be controlled for the benefit of all parties. If you're going to hire a comedian or controversial celebrity for a corporate event, they need to be told exactly what the boundaries are. Even with rules in place, they can still be very entertaining.

Binary Tree didn't just celebrate our team with lavish parties, we also shared profits. We would pay bonuses, even double bonuses, based on how well we had financially performed. Sure, some quarters dragged, but our team understood that if the company won, they won. That tempered the times when we couldn't quite share the wealth. In some ways, Binary Tree was business recession-proof. That didn't mean we couldn't fail. Rather, it meant that our team created an important product that nearly every single business out there needed. Email, as you can imagine, is the most mission-critical application for any company. It is budget proof. Without it, you couldn't communicate.

That is, in some ways, part of our recipe for success. We had a strong team and a rock-solid product and were market vital due to all the innovation and competition by the major players. By that I mean that the market had to welcome email evolution with new versions and new products. In doing so, they welcomed us, the company that would get them to "NEW." As one of the first companies to truly build a global brand around data migration, we were lucky enough to be recognized as one of the go-to companies to get the job done. That led to success, but oftentimes it also led to a tremendous amount of time away from my home and family.

Frequently, I was gone for several days or even weeks at a time. Because of all the time requirements at Microsoft headquarters near Seattle, I was often a five-hour flight from the people I loved the most. One trip would call me to Seattle for a Friday meeting, and I would have to be back there again for more meetings on Monday. It didn't make sense to travel home for forty-eight hours and then catch another cross-country flight from the East Coast. So, I tried to make the most of my time on the road, finding meaningful ways to spend the weekend.

These weekend layovers in the Pacific Northwest once took me to Mount Rainier, one of the most beautiful natural parts of the country. I decided to enjoy all that Mother Nature had to offer. My outings were extremely casual at first, but I started to go on longer weekend hikes, traversing many types of trails and terrain. I felt all kinds of release when I hiked, disconnected from the computer, cell phones, and the hustle and bustle of programming and running a business. I suppose it became a hobby of sorts, first out of the necessity to kill time and then out of pure love.

My first time hiking this remote, pristine environment, I followed the designated trail. Eventually, I encountered a sign that read, "No hiking past this point." For me, that was an invitation to break the rules to see what lay beyond the warning sign. This was in late spring, early summer, and the snow cover, ever present on Rainier, was increasing as I ascended the mountain. Everything I saw awed me. The curiosity and adventure got the better of me, and I continued to ascend.

As often occurs in the mountains, weather conditions rapidly changed. Fortunately, only fog set in, not a storm or something more serious. In my mind, I felt like I could not turn back. I had never seen nature in such a natural form, and I felt the need to continue to see more, thinking the path I left was an easy one to which I could return. I continued for about an hour, making a mental note of every remarkable spot to make turns on for my descent back to the sign I'd ignored.

When I got to the end of this tourist-forbidden section (a cliff with a deadly drop-off), I sat there in awe of my surroundings. Surprisingly, I had full cell service and called Larisa to share my experience with her. I'm pretty sure I was babbling and unable to find the proper vocabulary to describe my current location. I surely didn't share that I was off trail, on my own, on a cliff, with heavy fog settling in during the late afternoon. During the brief breaks in the fog and clouds encompassing the mountains, I saw the summit. It was inspiring, and I vowed that I would get there someday. I would soon learn that fateful summit is one of the highest peaks of the lower forty-eight states. However, due to its alpine-like conditions, constant crevasse danger, and highly variable weather, it is significantly more challenging to reach than many that are taller.

After I had my fill and realized the sun was quickly setting, I attempted to return to the trail and make my way to the trailhead. However, the fog was much thicker than I had anticipated, making it much more difficult to track the previous landmarks I had mentally recorded. But the fact that I still had cell service comforted me. I made several attempts on various paths and eventually succeeded in finding the other side of the No Hiking sign that I had previously ignored.

Slight drama aside, I fell in love with the peace you could find on a trail and then, much later, at the top of a mountain. As far as you could look, no one in sight. The warmth of the sun beating down on your back, the clouds in the sky taking form and morphing into different shapes that resembled everything from an animal to the perfectly etched silhouette of Italy or France. I got lost in those clouds time and time again, oftentimes simply sitting down to stare at them for a few minutes before carrying on with the trail.

In many ways, my time out there was both complementary to my burgeoning triathlon hobby and a stark contrast to my time in the office—the highs and lows, peaks and summits, and nearly everything in between. Out there, by myself, wasn't about pushing myself or setting a new personal best. Rather, it was about finding balance. Peace. Harmony. Synchronicity. Perhaps it was those afternoons or mornings on the mountains, or maybe just my time out of the office, but I found a love in movement both on a racecourse and alone in nature. Getting away from my desk and screen, to which I was attached for so long, and doing something to mix up the monotony of the tech game invigorated me.

I was not well-versed in the science behind how physical challenges and new experiences improve our overall well-being, both mentally and physically. I think I had a sixth sense that learning new, nonbusiness skills would help me survive the rat race I was participating in during the week. Who knew that these physical activities would improve creativity and empathy in my life and would also start playing a major role in it?

It was an escape of sorts, one that I didn't know I needed but that I welcomed through and through. Funny how the universe was planting seeds. I had put in the work for so long, and perhaps I needed to slow down. I repeatedly had that opportunity and found great adventures in going off trail in the US as well as memorable locations in Italy, Germany, Sweden, and other destinations work would take me. If it weren't for these hiking adventures and my recent triathlon racing hobby, I probably would have kept on the current path. But that wasn't the case, and something new came into my life. For so long, I was first in and the last out. That was my work ethic. That was the way I carried myself. Now, for the first time maybe ever, I was wondering if I could apply that same dynamic to something other than work . . . like more races and higher peaks.

Key Takeaways

- Make calculated decisions when choosing relationships between competing opportunities.

- Embed diversity and inclusion into your corporate culture as early as possible.

- Set clear expectations and limitations when inviting guest speakers and entertainers.

- Listen to that voice that tells you to take on a challenge that helps you balance your life.

PACE YOURSELF ON
AND OFF THE TRACK

IN MOUNTAINEERING, a porter helps carry gear up a mountain. They're often referred to as Sherpas, but technically that is only correct on Mount Everest. The Sherpa are a Tibetan tribe in the Himalayas, and every member's last name is, in fact, Sherpa. Often, they haul necessities like fuel, cooking gear, ropes, food, and tents. Most mountains require a certain ratio of porters to climbers as this is a main source of employment in some regions of the world. On Mount McKinley (also known as Denali) in Alaska, you and your team are the porters. More on that later.

When I got serious about climbing, we employed numerous porters to help us haul all our equipment and supplies. They were an integral part of our success and journey up any mountain. But more than the effort they put in to muscle up our essentials, they are wise beyond their years. They understand and respect the culture of the mountain and often offer wise feedback and insight to novice and even experienced climbers.

"Polay, polay," pronounced Pō-lā, is a phrase you hear often when climbing mountains in Africa. Translated, it means "slowly" in Swahili, a common phrase the porters often say to remind the anxious climbers to keep pace and never overexert. These two words often keep us grounded on and off treacherous mountain terrain. As a society, we have often programmed ourselves to put our heads down and move just as fast as we can, hardly worrying about what is ahead of us, what we left behind, or our ability to maintain an aggressive pace. While this might be sustainable for a short time, it often ends the same way—in failure.

Muscles, both mental and physical, can only handle so much. The more we push, the more likely we are to eventually reach full exhaustion and failure. You don't have to be on a mountain to recognize that. Binary Tree was growing rapidly. It was hardly steady. We were moving fast. At the time, that was the norm. Often, entrepreneurs feel the need to be incredibly disruptive and do it by moving as fast as humanly possible. They forget about what got them there, and they sacrifice quality for speed. This becomes a dangerous game that results in mistakes at best and complete meltdown at worst.

Of course, at times I felt myself moving too fast. And once you get a fast pace going, it is even harder to slow things down. No one wants to do the mundane work, only the growth work. There is no glory in balancing the books, paying taxes, submitting payroll, or saying no to potential sales. It is no fun to steadily move ahead, focusing on the repetitive steps that helped you build a strong foundation. Frankly, it is much more fun to sprint. Go until you can go no farther. But then what? When you fall flat on your face, exhausted, then what do you do?

I was fortunate to never really fall for this trap, and perhaps my activities out of the office helped me learn to avoid it. Looking for yet another outlet to break up the monotony of my swim/bike/run triathlon obsession, I became immersed in mountaineering, spending more and more time hiking and climbing on the weekends. It started as a welcome distraction while traveling in Washington and then Colorado and quickly became a sport for me, something I sought out on a regular basis. This magnificent release occurred when I was completely free, surrounded by the beauty of open terrain and a monster of a mountain under my feet while being disconnected from all stresses below. Standing at the base of something that large and just looking up at it inspires a remarkable feeling. It is breathtaking, inviting, and inspiring to think that I am going to begin a journey at the bottom of this granite beast and work my way to the top. Step after step, breath after breath, one foot in front of the other, powered only by physical ability and willpower to reach the top.

You never know what to expect when you are navigating a mountain. With each step comes a new risk, a small accomplishment, and an occasion to proceed or turn around. This is where pace comes in. It is not a race to the top. It is a journey to the top. The destination is simply reaching the summit. Move too fast, and your body will give up on you. Move too slow, and you will run out of time and supplies, and you will never make it. That is why you must maintain a moderate pace. Sure, things get harder as you get higher. It is much easier to keep moving in lower altitude settings. One step in front of the other seems like a relatively easy task. But, as you climb, higher and higher into the clouds, your pace needs to slow. At first, take one full breath in between steps and later two as you ascend. One step, two breaths. One step, two breaths. It can feel tedious, but your pace is often a product of your environment.

That is, sometimes there is value in moving fast. Other times, there is value in moving slow. Pace is not a speed. Rather, it is a situational response to the circumstances you face. I still remember, early on with Binary Tree, the dance of rolling out a new product or a new version of an existing one. Sure, you wanted to get it to market. But you wanted to go slow enough to make sure you addressed the big issues and fast enough so your competition didn't beat you to the punch. That is the balance of pace. It is never a constant for long. You must always make necessary adjustments to ensure you'll get where you need to be in a timely manner.

That is, at least in part, what I love about mountaineering. The mountain forces pace. It requires you to be aware of how slow or fast you are moving. In life, that is rarely true. Few elements cause such an awareness. In business, it is so easy to move fast—cash and your burn rate permitting, of course. Hardly any barriers exist to stop you. However, when mistakes creep in, things eventually fall apart and you are left trying to pick up the pieces. The only thing left to do at that point is to reflect, learn from what went wrong, and slow it down. But even then, business owners often double down and do things the same way all over again.

The mountain dictates the pace, not the other way around. That is how it should be, in and out of the office. Environmental factors should impose the appropriate speed and rate of movement, not the other way around. When it comes to you versus the mountain, the mountain will always win. It is undefeated. Every. Single. Time. A consistent, steady pace will win ten times out of ten. Then and only then will you be rewarded with the accomplishment of visiting its summit.

As we were building Binary Tree, moving from IBM to Microsoft and adding numerous other large companies to our ever-expanding rolodex, so to speak, it became clear that we could achieve wild success by maintaining the rhythm that got us there in the first place. Of course, I always wanted to speed it up. But I had surrounded myself with great people who, just like the porters on top of the mountain, reminded me to go slow.

Pace prevents burnout. It always has, and it always will. Often, burnout is the enemy of productivity. It stops you dead in your tracks, whether you are suffering from oxygen deprivation and muscle failure 15,000 feet above sea level on a mountain or hard-charging at the office, pulling all-nighters in hopes of servicing all the demands of the market. "*Polay, polay*" as the porters say. It is so easy to forget such a simple lesson, but it can absolutely be the difference in your sustainability and success.

Maintaining a steady pace is not always sexy. Trust me, you will want to speed it up, get to the next task, and put the current one in the rearview mirror. You might be scared that if you don't move fast, someone else will. A myriad of internal beliefs will cause you to feel the itchy need to move faster, rather than maintaining a consistent pace. But I can tell you from firsthand experience on and off the mountain, succumbing to these feelings is a mistake. It may seem gratifying at first, but that dopamine-induced high is only temporary. Eventually, it will all catch up with you. You cannot cheat the mountain. No way, no how.

It has taken me some time, but I have worked extremely hard to maintain a steady pace in my life. Even today, I find myself pushing too hard, going too fast, and having to take those deep breaths and slow it down. That is the best part about mountaineering—it forces your pace. Not the other way around. You don't tell the mountain who is the boss, the mountain tells you.

To ensure I maintain pace, I have worked on checking in with my body, listening to what it is telling me, and respecting what it says. My wife's parting words before any race or mountain adventure are "Have a great time. Listen to your body!" The body is a remarkable communicator, and it will quickly tell you when it feels good, bad, or nearly anything else. It will tell you to slow down, give you permission to speed up, and certainly let you know when it can take no more. Don't let it get to that point, like I have several times. Check in with yourself, and listen to the feedback you are receiving in response to your decisions and actions.

These measurements and key performance indicators will help you to run your business, your department, or even lead a small group to success. Analytics matter, and as they say, that which can be measured can be improved. Just like I repeatedly check in with my body during a race, every leader needs to check their business dashboard to ensure their team is moving towards the desired outcome and performance level. If not, checking in will help you to identify when you need to take corrective action. Showing a team objective data that supports a decision to act, goes a long way toward building confidence and support.

Focusing on my breathing helps me calm my feelings and maintain pace. It is relaxing and allows you to focus on something other than the notion that you must speed up. Your breath is a great indicator of your body's physical and mental state. The more you exert, the harder you breathe. The more duress you feel, whether mental or physical, the more rapid your breath will be. This is one of the greatest barometers available to you, and the more you tap into your breathing and listen to your breath, the better you can gauge your current state.

There should be no mystery about why one of the hardest yet greatest human feats is childbirth. Breathing is taught throughout the childbearing months. It is also integral to the magical birth event when it finally arrives. If it is integral and helpful to the most challenging event a human body can perform, imagine its benefits in other stressful situations.

Your company's cash is like oxygen to your body. Monitor it as closely as you possibly can and preserve it to the best of your ability. Because when you run out of it, you're in for some hurt. It continues to surprise me that some companies still have a hard time with cash flow projections. This is a combination of science and art, especially if you don't have predictable recurring revenue, but its importance cannot be overstated.

While your body can't flip a switch and get instant air, your company can get instant cash if you have the right debt facility available to you. Don't wait until you need it to establish a hefty credit line. Banks and regulations are tighter than they've ever been, and distressed companies will have a very hard time getting credit when they need it the most. Get credit when you're rocking your numbers and represent the least amount of risk to your bank. This also applies to your personal finances. I always have a home equity line or line of credit against assets readily available to tap into when needed.

Breathing is also an incredible tool to help get you into a desired mental or physical state. There are myriad techniques that can be very helpful. A lot has been published over the last few years on this topic. I've recently adopted the Wim Hof method and can't speak highly enough about it. One of the exercises he suggests in his book is to first establish your current pushup limit. Mine was thirty at the time. Then follow one of his breathing exercises for a few minutes and try again. I shocked myself by cranking out fifty pushups right afterwards.

I have found his breathing techniques to also be useful for dealing with cramps. These are inevitable when participating in endurance sports. They can be excruciatingly painful, stopping you dead in your tracks. I've had more than my fair share. After learning these new breathing techniques, mine go away almost as quickly as they appear.

Remain calm. Don't let others' pace dictate yours. It is a tortoise versus hare conversation. Slow and steady can absolutely win the race. This doesn't happen every single time, but you will find more consistency in your success when you go slow and focus on setting a steady pace that serves your best interests. This isn't a sprint. Few things are in life. Think about driving a car. I've always felt peace in hopping on the highway, putting on cruise control, and just maintaining a constant pace for the long journey ahead. There is no worse feeling than the start and stop of traffic, the slamming on your brakes, then your gas, then your brakes again. It is also bad for your car, messes with its mechanics, and burns gas at a much higher rate. Who wants to do that? Well, we can't control traffic, but we can absolutely control our pace in life.

My grandfather, may he rest in peace, continuously reminded me about this. He hated the way my uncle, laughing from heaven about this, would drive his car: hard acceleration followed by abrupt braking at the next light. My grandfather would reach over to me, stroke my arm, then lightly punch me as a comparison. I miss those moments.

The beauty of the concept of pacing is that you, and you alone, choose the right pace for you and your life. For your business. For your climbing. For nearly everything. You can move fast. Slow. Steady. But the one piece of advice I can give you, as you make that decision, is to listen to your body and consider environmental factors. If you are focusing on both the external and the internal factors, then you will be in the best position to make the most informed decisions and avoid burnout.

"Polay, polay" is the product of hundreds of years of climbing up the same mountain again and again. It is the function of many broken dreams, watching people attempt to summit a mountain and fail because they don't maintain the right pace. We can all benefit from slowing down just a little bit, assessing our pace, and adjusting to make sure we reach whatever summit we are chasing.

Key Takeaways

- Pace yourself in business and in life. Don't move so fast you get ahead of building a solid foundation.

- The mountain—the circumstance you face—dictates the pace.

- Repeatedly check your business dashboard to ensure your team is moving toward the desired outcome and performance level.

- Your company's cash is like oxygen to your body. Monitor it as closely as you possibly can and preserve it to the best of your ability.

MIND THE
SHORTCUTS

THERE ARE NO SHORT CUTS in endurance sports and adventures. As the name implies, you have to *endure*, and, in many cases, what you endure is time—a lot of it. On Mount McKinley in Alaska the distance between base camp and the summit is only 15.5 miles. Most people can speed walk that distance in about three hours. On McKinley, covering that distance requires over two weeks as you ascend 13,500 feet in altitude. It require days of acclimatization at various stages. Without giving your body a chance to increase its red blood cell count, you don't stand a chance of breathing properly, or of your body being able to handle the increased stress you're putting on it. There is no shortcut to the top.

Until I started a journey of great distance and meaning, shortcuts didn't matter much to me. I was perfectly fine staying the course and putting my head down. It just wasn't in my nature. When my family immigrated to the United States, they didn't have the chance or occasion to take any shortcuts. They navigated a new country, a new language, and new cultural norms day by day, hour by hour. If they weren't going to take any shortcuts, I wasn't going to either.

But shortcuts are funny. Even though you might pay them no attention at first, they eventually seem to be more and more attractive. The idea that you could shave a corner here, save a few hours there, or conserve money or effort can often seem too good to ignore. However, I have found out, sometimes the hard way, that taking the easy road leads to terrible outcomes.

It happened when we hired the first capable candidate we interviewed for an important position instead of taking our time and waiting for the best candidate. As you could likely guess, we usually had to replace them in the future. It happened when we rushed a product or new version of a product to market without all the necessary testing. Often, this created a scenario where our software had bugs and impacted customer satisfaction. It happened when we failed to document employee issues or have conversations with team members who didn't meet our expectations. That often led to eventual termination and likely could have been avoided had we properly addressed the issues at hand. At times, we also didn't fully document our strategies or approach to a project, expecting a team to execute without proper direction, resulting in missed expectations and frustration on both ends.

In each of these examples, we can easily see how shortcuts in the workplace can create significant and unnecessary pain and suffering. Hindsight is 20/20, and when you are in the heat of the battle, it is easy, maybe even predictable, that you will look for the easy way out. In the end, however, the easy way usually costs you dearly. It seems easy at the time but often costs twice as much in the long run. As they say, this behavior becomes pennywise and pound foolish. In fact, I bet I could say it again and again, but when the heat gets turned up, you are still going to look for the shortcut.

I don't blame you. It is human nature, embedded in our very DNA and existence. If the stove is hot, we take our hand off it. If the journey gets too cumbersome, we start squirming and looking around for a cheat sheet. It happens in nearly every part of our life. The shortcuts often happened first in business, but as I got more and more serious about pursuing marathon running, triathlons, and mountaineering, the shortcuts became even more glaringly apparent. After I started to race regularly, I decided to pursue similar endeavors that truly challenged the human spirit, mentally and physically.

When I fully invested in competing in triathlons, it was abundantly clear that I would have to exhibit some of the greatest discipline and dedication I could muster. This wasn't a small task, and it would require proper training and effort. Otherwise, my body would fail and wouldn't carry me to the finish line. To avoid the shortcuts, I started competing by signing up for something I thought was quite mundane compared to my goal: a half-marathon. It took some time and dedication, but I completed it. Next, I upped the ante and signed up to compete in an Olympic-distance triathlon. This was a beast, consisting of a mile swim, a twenty-five-mile bike ride, and a six-mile run. This would be the greatest challenge I had experienced to date. Also, as part of my training, I decided to run the New York City Marathon. I did this, in part, because I wanted to start training my body for longer distances and greater stress, but also because if I were to compete in an actual full-distance triathlon, I would have to run a marathon as part of it.

My wife and younger daughter came with me to Columbia, Maryland, for my first Olympic-distance triathlon. While at the registration tent, signing in for the race, Rochelle spotted a competitor and whispered to me, "Look, Dad, he's wearing an IRONMAN T-shirt!" She said it with such reverence that it further fueled my desire to race that distance someday. We also drove the bike course in our car so that I could get familiarized with the route. My wife said, "I don't know, Steven. This is very hilly. I don't have a good feeling about this." That was even more fuel for my fire.

Often, it took months to properly train for a race. Those months consisted of day after day of mundane routine. Ramping up, slowing down, recovering, medium-sized distances, long distances, days off, rinse and repeat. It was a war of attrition that occurred in my mind. As much as I wanted to hit race day and just compete, I knew the effort I expended each day would create the foundation any competitor needed to not just participate but thrive. At first, it was all about the destination. My mind was conditioned to look at the end and focus solely on that. But as I fully prepared my body for competition, I began to fall in love with the journey.

Sure, the destination was extremely important to me. It was the very reason I competed. I began to slow down, in body and mind, and realized that the journey was just as, if not more, special. I fell in love with the exercise, the training, the preparation for the actual race. The endorphin highs, the recovery lows. It all left a lasting imprint on my mind, one that stays with me to this day and often prompts my desire to get out of bed and train. As a competitor, you don't have to finish the game to feel a sense of accomplishment. A solid day of training would leave me feeling like I had accomplished something amazing during that short time.

It became something I chased each day and continue to reach for. The runner's high, as they call it. That shit is real! It took me over and was often the inspiration to get out of bed on those dreadfully dark and cold mornings and put in the work. I couldn't get enough. The journey is an awesome one. That seems to be the case in building anything that matters. Training for a triathlon or other substantial race reminded me a lot of building Binary Tree. No days off. Endless energy and effort. Of course, no shortcuts. Every single day. Laying bricks, one after the other. That is the only way you can build a lasting foundation for anything that really matters.

The funny thing about building a foundation is that your effort and energy in doing so will either create something that lasts or result in it all crumbling down. You can't cheat physics. Strong foundations support large amounts of weight. A weak foundation will inevitably crumble under similar circumstances. You must take methodical, strategic steps to build for the future. You can either put in the effort of building it or put in twice as much effort picking up the pieces and rebuilding it when it all comes tumbling down.

Shortcuts are everywhere, whether you are building a company or training for a race. It is easy to take a day off, to cut corners on your financial reports, to forego that last mile on a hot day to cool your muscles down before ending a workout, to under-hire to save a few bucks. Each of these practices can often create small but lasting cracks in the foundation. The cracks always build up. It may not be the first shortcut or even the tenth one that caused a horrible outcome, but dozens of small cracks can weaken the foundation to the extent that it just cannot bear weight. That is when disaster strikes. Many people subscribe to the false notion that there is always time to do something twice, but there's rarely time to do it right the first time. They rush through important tasks just to get them done, accepting the fact that they'll almost certainly have to do them again. In the moment, and in that sense of instant gratification, it feels like the right thing to do. However, future outcomes will often act as reminders of past mistakes.

We compared business competitors to fragile houses of cards. While they seem attractive and elegant on the outside, it usually takes little effort for them to fall apart. Just go after the weakest link, and the rest won't be able to sustain the outside structure. People have said the same thing about Binary Tree, but it was wishful thinking on their part, at least most of the time.

In the end, shortcuts catch up with you every single time. Don't hydrate, and you get cramps. Don't put enough calories in your body, and it will give out on you. Don't train your muscles to experience and understand fatigue, and you'll never find yourself capable of fighting through atrophy. Shortcuts not only create chinks in your armor, but they also prevent you from fully understanding how to fight through failure. When you constantly take shortcuts, you begin to cheat your full potential. There is no substitute for hard work, and shortcuts simply cut some of the hard work you have to do to reach your goals.

I have always thought of shortcuts as the act of doing the least amount of possible work to get a desired outcome. Remember, not all outcomes are the same. Sometimes, just getting to the finish line is good enough. I wouldn't be where I am today if I took every single shortcut that presented itself. Trust me, there were many. When you go on a journey as long as mine, and do it again and again, it is truly remarkable how many opportunities to save time and resources present themselves. They are literally everywhere. Boy, are they tempting.

That is not to say that every single shortcut has a negative connotation or outcome. Just look at artificial intelligence as an example of a shortcut that can save you valuable time and resources, and potentially help you get the job done better than you could on your own. I am a huge proponent for the use of shortcuts to make your life easier. However, you can't let it compromise the quality of the result. One of the greatest qualities any leader can develop is the ability to save time and money. No doubt, it is a necessary part of leadership. We all want to build lean and mean companies that carry little, if any, waste. You do that by finding ways to automate tasks that humans would otherwise have to do. You do that by finding creative ways to save money through trimming overhead and optimizing your business.

But all shortcuts aren't created equal. Some are amazing hacks that can help you excel. Others are poisonous fruits that might appear to be attractive but will inevitably cost you dearly. I have always been one to trust my gut when it comes to picking and choosing the shortcuts to take and those to pass. It takes time to do that. It takes trial and error. Sometimes, it takes learning a valuable lesson to later decide that your shortcuts aren't the right ones.

From firsthand experience, trust your gut. No better measuring stick exists to ensure you are picking and choosing the right type of shortcut. If it feels too good to be true, then it probably is. Shortcuts often save a small amount of time, money, and other valuable resources. They rarely reinvent the wheel. If they do, be very careful that you aren't cutting the wrong types of corners. We see that occur every single day, particularly in the finance sector—failing to report accurate earnings, inflated books, understated risks, insider trading, and so on. These are the types of corners you just simply cannot cut. Your gut knows it's wrong. You know when you are being unethical and dishonest. Shortcuts should maintain the same level of accountability and integrity that doing it the right way would. Remember, there are places to cut corners and there are other places where you simply cannot.

Don't cut corners in the way you treat people. Maintain integrity and honesty in business and in your personal life. These are places where shortcuts have no business. The better you know yourself, the better you can assess where and how to use a shortcut. Some people prefer to play it by the book. Others are willing to take logical risks to get substantial returns. Shortcuts are hardly one-size-fits-all. In fact, a shortcut for one person may just be the usual way of doing it for another. Do not allow others to push you outside of your comfort zone and pursue shortcuts you wouldn't otherwise feel comfortable taking.

The term "quality time" is a kind of shortcut and an expression that irks me. Sure, there are business examples of great outcomes that leaders can achieve with very little expenditure of time with others. What I hate is when that is applied to family and friends. In that instance, there is no substitute for quantity of time with them. Long car rides, endless hours on the beach, spending time outdoors, or playing a board game with family is when we make true memories. That's probably the single best thing to come out of the recent pandemic. Some of the most hysterical and memorable moments I've had with my daughters are during ten-plus-hour drives to and from college; the same with my wife on numerous road trips through Arizona, Nevada, and Utah. Sure, we could have flown there much quicker, but I wouldn't trade the memories we've built for anything. Same with friends. Most restaurants turn their tables in sixty to ninety minutes. Good luck getting a table of me, my wife, and a group of our friends out in under four hours. We'll usually close down any place we visit, and that's the way it should be. At least we tip well.

Whether it's running, biking, swimming, building a business, being a parent, husband, son, friend, or nearly anything else I am or I do, short-cuts are ever-available. I have always tried to look at them like salt—know that a little can go a long way. Some of the shortcuts I've taken have helped me reach great levels of success. Others have taught me lessons, sometimes the hard way. My awareness around shortcuts gives me the greatest opportunity to use them or not.

I didn't know it at the time, but training for triathlons and ultra-marathons would teach me more about shortcuts than nearly any other experience. They taught me that shortcuts can eventually cause you to completely fall short of your goal. They taught me that there is no substitute for hard work. They taught me that it can be tempting to pursue shortcuts, but it takes twice as much time to recover from a botched shortcut than it does to just do things right the first time. Oh, the lessons I've learned. Perhaps the most important one is that we all do things in different ways. No two paths are the same, and the more we realize that we must take the path and journey that is the best fit for us, the less likely we will care to even consider cutting corners.

Key Takeaways

- You can't cheat physics. Strong foundations support large amounts of weight.

- Not all outcomes are the same. Just getting to the finish line is often good enough.

- Use the shortcuts that make your life easier as long as you don't sacrifice quality.

- Never shortcut people. Honesty, integrity, and spending time with people you care about should never be short-changed.

NOT FAST,
NOT LAST

AS I CONTINUED to run longer and longer distances and push my body to the extreme, I coveted greater challenges and additional opportunities to truly test my limits. One marathon turned into many, and running soon turned into biking and swimming as well. I found the different disciplines quite attractive, each one testing a different skill set or helping me develop a different type of mental fortitude. They say you never forget your first race, and that was certainly true, but eventually I needed something that challenged me in a different way. It didn't take long to find that prospect—full-distance triathlon.

One of the most significant and taxing things you can do to your body and mind, a full-distance triathlon is a 2.4-mile swim, followed by a 112-mile bike ride, topped off with a full marathon, coming in at 140.6 total miles for the day. Some would say you'd have to be completely batshit crazy to take on a beast like this, and well, I would tend to agree. But I set my sights on it, and I was ready to aim and fire.

Training for a triathlon is unlike anything else. When I learned about IRONMAN Lake Placid, which is close to my home, I decided this would be my first full-distance challenge. Just under five hours away, Lake Placid is a historic location—host to the Olympics, site of the Miracle on Ice, and a training epicenter for many athletes. Leading up to the event, I trained hard. Real hard.

We are talking about twenty-plus-hour weeks of training, consisting of long swims, bike rides, and, of course, runs. This was on top of a fifty- to sixty-hour workweek. I wasn't the fastest guy around, but I was dedicated to the process, and I put in the work.

In the first six months of 2011, leading up to that race, I totaled 77 miles of swimming, 2,986 miles on the bicycle, and 509 miles of running in preparation for this milestone. This called for a lot of early morning workouts and long weekend rides and runs. While laborious at times, I enjoyed the journey and always felt inspired upon completing a long bike ride or run.

They say the finish line is the true destination, but I found that the journey is perhaps the most special part. In some ways, preparing for the event is a tremendous war of attrition, waking up every single day and demanding so much of your body and mind. Training for half a day gives you a lot of time to think. And that is what I did. I thought a lot about the challenge of training, the somewhat redundant process of pushing your mind and body well past their normal thresholds. I thought about how I could sustain my training and how to get past the atrophy, the boredom, and the exhaustion.

It became a pretty regular conversation with my friends. Fascinated by my goal, or just presuming I had gone nuts, they often inquired about how I would get through it. At first, I didn't have an answer. But, eventually, perhaps after a long day of training that truly left me bruised and battered, I looked at one of my friends and said, "Not fast, not last." It just sort of came out. I even paused when I said it, mostly because it encompassed exactly what I was trying to do.

I didn't have to finish fast or first. I just didn't want to finish last. When you are competing at that level, only a few dozen of the two thousand people racing are competing against anyone other than themselves. Most of us are just trying to push our bodies and minds to an unfathomable goal. Sure, we all care about our time. If you want to compete in the coveted IRONMAN World Championship in Kona, you have no choice but to make the cut. But that doesn't mean you have to finish first either. The old joke goes, "What do you call the medical student who finishes last in his class?" The answer: "Doctor!" The same is true in triathlons. Everyone completing the course before the cutoff time gets a coveted Finisher Medal. Completing the race is an entirely spectacular accomplishment in itself. Perhaps I knew I wasn't going to be at the top of the leaderboard, but that didn't stop me from setting personal goals and working to always finish faster and stronger.

I started competing in my forties, so I wasn't exactly a spring chicken. I had some miles on these legs, and no one considered me an elite athlete. Probably fewer than a hundred people compete in triathlons for a living. They are the folks who have the sponsorships and enjoy the prize money. Let me be clear: Steven Pivnik is not one of these people. Very few of us reach the finish line and say, "What is my number?" Hell, we are just happy to be alive.

Something special occurs when you train for the grandaddy of all triathlons. Your body and mind transform. They become stronger, more agile, durable, and almost like a machine. You begin to fire on all cylinders, pistons pumping and the raw iron of your DNA propelling you toward your goal. Eventually, as you move farther down the race, your body begins to break down. That is a natural reaction to the stress your muscles experience. The atrophy sneaks into your quads, spreads to your hamstrings, your calves, and like poison running through your veins, touches every single inch of your entire being.

Things get real tough real quick. You almost have to trick your mind to believe it can keep going. To fight off failure. To finish . . . not fast, but not last either. When I cemented this as my slogan for racing, things started to change for me. There wasn't this incessant voice in my head telling me to keep going faster. Rather, I was able to push my own boundaries, compete against the limiting beliefs that stood in my way, and create a healthier and more successful journey to the finish line. It was an epiphany of sorts—one that sticks with me to this day.

You see, this concept has far-reaching implications. Far too many people look with tunnel vision at the finish line. That is the target. Nothing more. In doing so, they fail to recognize the importance and value of the journey and road ahead. No competitor that looked just to the finish line ever made it there in one piece. And if you do make it, there is a tendency to look back and critique the journey. How can I shave ten minutes off my bike ride? Five minutes off my run? Seconds off the swim? What you should really be considering is how remarkable the task you just completed is, how the journey led you to the destination.

Business trained me to recognize that magic happens in the trenches, not at the finish line or in the corner office. In my professional world, I always presumed you were either first or last. Because I rolled up my sleeves so often and spent time on real-life projects at customer locations, I was able to create unique solutions and customer outcomes with my team based on real-world scenarios. We invented several of our cutting-edge differentiators in the trenches. This brought us to the front of the thought leadership position in our market.

We built a successful company off leading the charge. And if one of our competitors started to catch up with us, then we charged ahead. Faster, stronger, bigger, and better. If not first, then worst. Coming from that type of battle zone, it wasn't always easy to shift my mindset to an entirely different approach to competing. "Not fast, not last" surely isn't for everything or for everyone, but it can make a substantial difference when you are competing against no one but yourself. We are always our own greatest opponent.

In the business world, it is often easy to compete against yourself when, for example, you are asked for a "better price" on a product or service you offer. Providing a better price when you are aware that a competitor is underbidding you is one thing, and it should be addressed strategically. Offering a better price when no competition is mentioned or known of is one step towards the slippery slope of competing against yourself. A firm but polite no goes a long way in this scenario. "Sorry, Ms. Customer. I provided a fair price in my proposal and I'm afraid I'm going to have to stick to it." Few business owners will have the confidence to provide that response and will often give a concession in price. Smart buyers on the customer's side know and expect this.

Saying no doesn't come without risk. Many years back, we decided to investigate getting a pool for our backyard. A reputable company gave me a proposal of $55,000 after hearing our requirements. Being the negotiator that I am, I said that he would have a deal at $50,000. He provided the answer I suggested above, and I told him I would think about it. By refusing to negotiate, he lost my business, and we never did get a pool.

I attribute my lack of injuries to the not-fast, not-last mindset. In endurance sports, injuries are quite common. Shin splits, runner's knee, Achilles tendinitis, IT band syndrome, and plantar fasciitis are just a few that I often hear about. When talking to others and getting asked about injuries, most are quite surprised when I just shake my head and say, "No, I haven't had any of those." I'm thrilled with getting to the finish line. I may get there a little slower than others, but I do it without paying that painful price.

The same can be said for business. I read a lot, and I get many great ideas from business books, but I'm hesitant to bring each and every idea into the business too often. This is because I try to avoid having my team's heads spin with continuous new initiatives. Similarly, I've seen leaders come up with bright and shiny objects that took their team's focus away from their current strategic initiatives. "Polay, polay" would be a good one to use here when you encounter this.

The art of slowing down is a special skill set. It isn't easy. In a world that values instant gratification and moving on to the next thing, speed is key. But speed doesn't always equate to a positive outcome. In fact, sometimes your speed can cause you to fail, to fall short of your goals, or to conk out before you hit the finish line. Not fast, not last.

Now, armed with a mantra that would carry the day, I was ready for IRONMAN Lake Placid. I invited my sister and her family to join my own family, hoping I wouldn't embarrass myself or my growing fan section waiting for me at the finish line. The race was grueling, Lake Placid being a particularly challenging venue. It is a super hilly bike course with over 4,000 feet of elevation gain and a good number of hills on the run, with 1,600 feet of elevation gain for the marathon.

We started the race at dawn. The water was brisk, and my wet suit stuck to me like glue. It seemed like it took forever, and it nearly did, but I recall turning one corner on the run and seeing the Olympic Oval in plain view marking the finish line. I was exhausted, falling apart, ready to throw in the towel. But then, as the sun set into a beautiful orange, purple, and blue sky, I knew I was close. I could hear the announcer, his voice loudly proclaiming to a fellow competitor, "Joe Smith, congratulations. You are an IRONMAN!"

My entire family cheering me on in a line as I edged closer to completing my first long distance triathlon seemed like a mirage at first. I was steps away from the finish line, and the announcer said, "Steven Pivnik, congratulations. You are an IRONMAN!" In that moment, I felt euphoric. It was monumental to me. I had done it. My family embraced me as I nearly collapsed into their arms. Thirteen hours and thirty-one minutes! My time shocked me. It shocked my coach. I had crushed the seventeen-hour cutoff finishing time.

As I stood at the finish line, marinating in the moment, I knew I had done something special. Something few people could add to their name. "Steven Pivnik, you are an IRONMAN!" replayed in my head. Not in a cheesy way. In a "Holy shit! I can't believe I just set out to do that and did it" type of way. As I looked back toward the finish line, I rejoiced to see other competitors completing the race. *Not fast, not last*, I thought. In spite of my programming to go, go, go, I was able to slow it down and do the work. I had set a goal and patiently worked toward it.

In life, we often feel like winning is the most important thing. Training and competing in triathlons will quickly teach you that participating, not winning, is really the finish line. I was fortunate enough to learn that the easy way. I didn't have to fall short of the finish line to realize that the only person I have to prove myself to is . . . well . . . myself.

But participating is not solely for racing. Think about all the other areas of our lives that we can celebrate participation. The area of spirituality comes to mind. You never become a spiritual expert. There is no finish line. Rather, we embark on an endless and rewarding journey to simply do better, find deeper spirituality and connection, and seek happiness and meaning in life.

Remember, "not fast, not last" means that you don't have to always let the end dictate your success. You are enough just because you completed the journey. First, second, or next to last, you did it. It took competing in this punishing event for me to realize that. If I was going to base my success on my placement, I would overlook the greatest success of all: getting to the end.

Key Takeaways

- Value the journey, not just the destination.
- The magic happens in the trenches, so roll up your sleeves and pitch in.
- You can make a substantial difference when you consider yourself your greatest competition.

OVERTRAINING
SYNDROME

THERE ARE TIMES FOR PACING YOURSELF, and there are times for pushing yourself, especially when there is a prize in sight.

We have all been there—pushing too hard, extending too much, or taking that one extra costly step. In a word, overtraining—making your body go past the point of healthy failure and landing at the doorstep of injury. Unfortunately, for anyone preparing for and training for a triathlon or an ultramarathon, overtraining syndrome is real and gets you when you least expect it. These races call for intensive training, pushing yourself well past the point of normal human tolerance. As you can imagine, a thin line exists between getting ready for a race and overdoing it. You have to walk that line each and every time, knowing that crossing it can have dire consequences.

After finishing my first full-distance triathlon, I felt an incredible sense of accomplishment. It was an immediate new addiction, a rush of energy and feel-good hormones that I knew I wanted to feel again and again. They say you'll always remember the first time you cross the finish line, and I finally knew what they meant. I couldn't wait to be there again. Even though I set my sights on competing in Kona one day, I knew there would be many stops on this journey to Hawaii. When I arrived home after IRONMAN Lake Placid, I had a new energy about me. Some would call it Type A on steroids, as I now had this remarkable rush of inspiration that began to carry me through my personal and professional life.

The tagline for IRONMAN is "Anything Is Possible™." I don't think I really knew what that meant until I finished my first race. If I wasn't drinking the Kool-Aid before that event, I was surely drinking it afterward. In some ways, I felt this renewed sense of possibility at work, as if I could do nearly anything; pushing my staff to set more challenging goals, recognizing that we couldn't settle for our then-current accolades, and constantly pushing the envelope of products and customer service—there were so many ways we could do more.

We were expanding into Europe at the time I finished IRONMAN Lake Placid, and that motivated me to press even harder than usual. Together, my team and I set pretty audacious sales targets, knowing they might be out of reach but refusing to settle for average. Binary Tree expanded its hiring practices, our staff, and our relationships with other partners, and we decided to go after some of the biggest systems integrators to resell our products. Our attitude? There was no reason for companies like HP, Dell, Avanade, and others to use our competitors' products. We were the alpha dog, and we would show them why.

There were definitely times when we overtrained and set ourselves up for financial failure. We strained our cash and resources at times by going after quantity and not focusing on quality. We executed a great strategy by expanding into France, but failed to gain similar traction in an even larger market like Germany. We made great progress with some systems integrators while spinning our wheels with others.

I've found that Americans usually underestimate the difficulty of international expansion. For this example, even with my Eastern European heritage, I'll throw myself into that bucket. We grouped most of the world outside of the United States into the EMEA (Europe, Middle East, and Asia) category. There are 115 counties in that group! While Americans don't necessarily mind buying from a different state, there are many different cultures to deal with abroad. They are very appreciative and often respectful of their cultural differences from us, but still honor their own preferences. We were successful in France because we had an entire team there. A customer in France dealt with a French salesperson, a French technical solutions architect, a French implementation consultant, and so on. That combination delivered superior results, but a customer located in Italy who received sales, technical support, and services from our employees in other countries had a different experience.

From a reseller and systems integrator perspective, we thought we would have the same level of success of displacing our competition by approaching these companies from either the top down at an executive level or bottom up from a technical field resource perspective. After months and sometimes years of effort, the latter proved to be much more effective. Those were the feet on the street performing the work and being held accountable for customer satisfaction.

We did a lot of things right and learned many lessons by doing some things wrong. Even so, by 2011, we enjoyed and sustained a good deal of personal and professional growth. In some ways, we were on autopilot, but I knew the importance of constantly checking in with my mind and body. Perhaps that is one of the greatest lessons you learn when competing in a multisport endurance event. You aren't an autonomous car, created to simply go without forethought. When you are training for something as significant as a triathlon, it is not just practical but absolutely necessary to listen to your body, especially when you are new to the competition. And it's the same in business. You have to listen to your customers and your employees on the ground. They are the heartbeat of your company.

When I trained for my first full-distance triathlon, I was almost obsessed with following a specific training regimen. I hired a coach and followed his plan religiously, day by day, almost hour by hour. I didn't miss a session, and it was like coloring by numbers for me. I think that is often the case for most first-time competitors. However, as you experience something new and it becomes more familiar, there is a tendency to get comfortable and feel like you can adjust and make changes. That's where you can get into trouble.

It's important to trust the process because you as the competitor or business owner have to maintain faith that what you are doing is good enough. It's not easy to trust without seeing—to blindly assume you are doing the right thing without instant results. It is more like faith than anything else. We live in a world with a tendency to overdo nearly everything. It is so common. We overdrink, overeat, overcomplicate, overthink, and overwork. So rarely do we recognize someone for over-loving, over-delivering, or for being overnice.

Training for a triathlon is a rhythmic exercise. You almost get into a flow of sorts, and you find yourself knee-deep in the three disciplines. If you're smart, you stick to the training plan. If you can afford it, you get a trainer and follow their lead. That will help you improve your muscles, your stamina, and your ability. But it's very easy to overdo it as well. Your body needs, even requires, specific breaks from each discipline. I added an extra run here or there, knowing I needed to trim my time. While I was fortunate enough not to do any permanent damage to myself, it caused problems.

It took longer to recover. I felt more fatigue, and you know what . . . my running time didn't improve. In fact, I lost two runs the next week just recovering from my overtraining. Muscles get stronger when they rest. Sure, it is your responsibility to train to failure, exhausting them and causing them to fatigue. But we get stronger when we recover, not when we perform. In some ways, it's the opposite of being lazy. In fact, it's kind of arrogant. You don't know more than the next guy. And you certainly don't know more than your muscles. They will be clear with you, telling you when they've had enough.

Another parable to my European expansion example is the concept of chiefs and warriors. This is an analogy often used for hiring more managers versus staff. Executives versus Field Resources. Thinkers versus Doers. This is also a classic case of overdoing it on the management front and understaffing on the roles that will actually get the ideas and work accomplished. There was a great UPS commercial by MullenLowe that parodied this concept. Two consultants were wrapping up a big pitch to their executive client with ". . . We think you need to integrate your global supply chain, move assembly overseas, and accelerate inventory velocity." After a deep breath the client smiles and says, "Great. Do it!" The consultants, almost in shock, respond with "Sir, we don't actually do what we propose. We just propose it." The commercial ends with the consultants walking out of the building saying, "Can you believe that guy?"

When your field resources are sending up signals for assistance due to work overload, these messages should be taken seriously and acted upon, just like when your muscles are telling you that you've been overtraining. Not making changes is not a good idea.

It is admirable to train hard and work tirelessly to succeed. That, in and of itself, should be celebrated. But it should also be tempered. There are numerous videos of competitors crawling, literally, to the finish line, or throwing in the towel before they get there. In the end, they end up foregoing the ability to compete because they thought they could play around and do just a little bit more than the next person. That dedication is what got us there in the first place. I love that part about myself. However, that is what makes it so much harder to find the right balance in your life.

Balance is key. I cannot overstate the negative impact and diminished returns of overtraining syndrome. It can happen in nearly every part of our lives. In many ways, our world pushes us to never rest until we collapse. The old saying "I'll sleep when I'm dead" seems to creep into the conversation. That is the unhealthy attitude to which we subscribe. We can't help ourselves. If we don't push it to the max, then we risk failing. What a horrible way to live!

It is admirable to work hard, train hard, set lofty goals, and fight like hell to achieve them each and every day of your life. As I see it though, there must be balance. When you are out of balance and your life lacks harmony, you'll likely feel the pain of pushing it. It is quite simple to avoid overtraining syndrome. Well, *simple* in the sense that it isn't terribly hard to understand how to avoid it. However, it isn't always easy to make the right choice. So, how do we do it? Slow. It. Down. There—easy right? Let me tell you that it takes just as much discipline to slow down as it does to train hard each day. The same freaking muscles. That is what makes this so interesting.

Your mind can either be a force that pushes you to overtrain or a calming guide to help you find the best pace. The more you check in with yourself and listen to your body, the better. You're not going to miss the race because you sit out a run or a bike ride. But you might miss the race if you suffer a long-term injury because you overtrain. Just consider the risk versus reward here. Do that, and it is an easy decision. Whether it is racing or living, you can implement best practices to stay the course and maintain your success. Focus on building those habits and repetitiously hitting your goals. Don't deviate. Don't make excuses. Don't explain your behavior away.

I once heard a racer say, "You're either overtraining or not training at all."

Poor guy, he didn't have a clue.

Key Takeaways

- Doing more doesn't always give you more. Resist the urge to overextend yourself in business and in life.

- Balance the quantity of great ideas and advice with your ability to implement them.

- Listen to the signals that bubble up from the heart of your business . . . or the heart of you.

ABC
(ALWAYS BE CLOSING . . .
YOUR BOOKS)

ULTRAMARATHON RACES can be thirty-two to a hundred miles long, sometimes even longer. Thus, you must pace yourself for the long journey ahead. Most racers do this by having a nutrition plan and knowing exactly the amount of calories they're going to need to support their bodies through such a strenuous experience. As you prepare for the race, most racers will compile these necessities and put them in bags. We refer to these as "drop bags." Drop bags are strategically placed among multiple aid stations along the race course.

We often put supplements, gels, water, electrolytes, a change of socks or sneakers, extra pants or shorts, and several other crucial resources we might need. If the race lasts into the night, we might also include some headlamps, batteries, and reflectors. To plan out these bags and the corresponding nutrients you might need, you have to consider carefully and plot out the map of the course. Poor planning can cause you to fail or DNF (Did Not Finish), but it can also be extremely dangerous to lack essential nutrition, a change of clothes, or safety devices like headlamps. You consume a tremendous amount of calories over the course of a super race like this, and your body will simply shut down on you if not cared for. It is nearly impossible to take in more calories than you burn, so we rely heavily on dense calories like PB&J sandwiches, Snickers, and Twizzlers.

When I think about the preparation it takes to plan for a race, or similarly a mountaineering expedition, it absolutely reminds me of closing your business books. They both rely on the same standard of planning and plotting out your journey.

When I was building and growing Binary Tree, I recognized the importance of always being ready for anything. Whether it was a new prospect, occasion for growth, or break in the tides of the technology or business industry, you never knew when luck or opportunity would appear. But one thing I did know is that when either did, you had to grab it by the horns, wrestle it to the ground, and make it your own. You never get a second chance to make a first impression, and you never get a second opportunity to close a lucrative deal.

At Binary Tree, we often had to work closely with banks and vendors to open and manage large lines of credit. We would then use the lines and our trusted purchasing power to secure resources like additional staff and technology—the things we needed to operate and grow our business. On many occasions, we felt the squeeze of the finances and had to ask our lenders for more time, more money, or greater flexibility. When I left and later returned to Binary Tree, I had to go to every single bank we worked with to renegotiate our debt. Often, the first thing they requested was to inspect our books.

In many ways, your books, or your financial records, represent the health of your company. The balance sheets, P&L reports, sales numbers, and other financial statements are all indicators of where you have been, where you currently stand, and, of course, where you might be headed. Most business owners are not always disciplined enough to focus their attention on the books. Frankly, it is easy to fall behind in this area, and many companies do.

In working with numerous business endeavors, I've seen just how liberal leadership can be with their books. Often, they let them go untouched for months, waiting until the end of the year to gauge the health or pulse of their business. This is a horrible mistake which often leads to catastrophes. In the wise words of Peter Drucker, "You can't manage what you don't measure."

The more attention you pay to your books, the better off you and your company will be. It is like taking care of your lawn. You can tell a lot about a homeowner by how they keep up their yard. A perfectly manicured lawn would lead you to believe the homeowner cares deeply about his or her house and likely takes care of the inside of it as well. They take pride in its appearance and are likely a good neighbor. Compare their house to one with a sloppy lawn, riddled with weeds and overgrown shrubs. You might conclude a homeowner like this does not give a shit.

To make matters even more complicated, think about how hard it is to sift through a lawn or garden that has grown over for years on end versus one that just needs a weekly touchup. Which one would be easier for the homeowner? The more we take care of ourselves and our possessions, the easier it is to remain ahead of the game. Your books are the exact same way. For the most part, they are relatively easy to manage when you deal with them regularly. Entering a few weeks of numbers is much easier than entering numbers for several months or an entire year.

Closing the books, above all else, makes your life easier in the long run. It indicates a strong discipline and maturity. It shows a dedication to remaining ahead of the game and being prepared for when opportunity comes knocking, or when it's time to knock on doors, cap in hand. The banks we were asking to give us more money or flexibility had good reason to ask to see our books. They will never just take your word for it, they will always base their decision on the financials.

Guess what? It didn't take but a few hours to get them all they needed to make an informed decision. That showed the banks we were serious about turning things around, and we were organized enough to do so. We made a great first impression as the banks then perceived that we were under different management and things would steadily improve. Had I taken days or weeks to get them our financials, I can only imagine how they would have reacted.

Everyone on your executive team should have a thorough understanding of the books. It shouldn't be a mystery but rather transparent and clear. These key performance indicators are constant reminders of the trajectory of your business. Interestingly enough, closing your books also requires a steady dose of organization, inner-office communication, a focus on your key performance indicators, studying your cashflow, and constantly looking toward the future. The books bring people together as it takes more than just one finance guy in a back corner office to get the job done.

Closing the books forces you to study every element of the business, inside and out. For a business to run well, each and every team member must do their job. They should know what the company needs, what the other departments need, and, of course, what the CEO needs. This synergy helps create a healthy, interactive environment with collaborative efforts that raise the tides across the board. A successful business is the culmination of tons of effort and attention to detail. From the CEO to the website manager, each and every professional must do their job. That is why closing the books is crucial to success. It offers both a macro and a micro view of your company.

When we took a deep dive into Binary Tree, I found that studying our books helped show what each part of the company was doing with its time and resources. It helped us see where we could improve, where we were excelling, and how we could adjust to maximize our earning potential. Your books can help you prioritize what is crucial, what can wait until later, and what should be on the list for your future. The books can assist you in every department of your company in recognizing if the numbers support your feelings about the health of your business.

We didn't always close our books at Binary Tree on a regular basis. But especially as we grew, I made it a specific deliverable of each department. They all had to own their books. Religiously. Weekly. This was going to be part of their job description, period. My team bought in. They began to see the value in constantly monitoring the numbers, of being so far ahead of the game that we always knew where we were and where we were heading. There was no reason not to remove the mystery from it all. Cold, hard numbers would dictate whether people remained on, were let go, or got raises. I found it to be a much easier way to manage because there was absolute transparency. Everyone knew where we stood.

Closing the books became a thing well before I started to compete in triathlons, but I think my colleagues and team would tell you that I really ramped it up afterward. It takes tremendous discipline and planning to compete in triathlons, more than I could have ever imagined or would have cared to invite into my life. But when you hit that finish line, you understand exactly why that discipline and focus on details is critical to your accomplishment. I closed my metaphorical books each week in training. You see, after a rigorous week of swimming, cycling, and running, I would look back at my notes, my schedule, and my times, determining what I did right, what I did wrong, and what I could improve.

Then, in starting the next week, I could make thoughtful adjustments to ensure I maximized my training moving forward. This simple act of measurement forced me to be strategic in all that I did. If I was going to travel, I needed to find a hotel with a pool. If I was going to be out of pocket all day at a meeting, I had to carve out time to run. If I missed a training session or had to cut one short the previous week, it was imperative that I adjust to ensure that it didn't happen again. The only way to accomplish this high level of training is to close your books each week.

Closing your books isn't always simple, yet it's one of the greatest examples of the value in being extremely disciplined and organized. It is a learned art form and easy to cheat over time. But the books never lie, and you will always be a product of that series of numbers. The more you close your books and the more races you run, the better you can be equipped to plan for the next journey or challenge. The more we know, the more we measure, and the more we study, the more adept we are at succeeding, whether it be in business or in racing.

In both my business and my training, I developed a renewed attitude and discipline during this time. I could do more than ever before, and I was recognizing a high level of productivity. I was on a mission to get to Kona, but I had to first knock out race after race, hoping to build up my stamina to keep competing. I completed IRONMAN

Kärnten-Klagenfurt, Austria, and then IRONMAN Arizona. They were brutal but remarkably rewarding. Training six to eight months for one day of sheer intense challenge wasn't always easy, but I was devoted to doing it again and again.

However, as I applied a great deal of discipline and organization to my training, I managed to navigate it with the least amount of pain and struggle. Always. Be. Closing. Your. Books. This is a simple yet powerful lesson. Most people learn it the hard way. A lost opportunity. A government audit. An employee stealing from their organization. Very few, if any, learn the value of closing their books without the occurrence of a significant event. I was one of the lucky ones, and you can be too.

Key Takeaways

- Take pride in the details and, if you are running a business or own a home, tend to your lawn every single day.

- Closing the books forces you to study every element of the business, inside and out.

- The discipline of closing the books will help you be ready when opportunity knocks.

12

THE LEGACY LOTTERY

THE LOTTERY TO COMPETE in the IRONMAN World Championship, created in 1983, was the brainchild of Judy and John Collins, the founders of the event. Judy and John have a unique story, moving from California to Hawaii in 1975 after competing in the Mission Bay Triathlon in San Diego in September of the previous year. In 1975, they helped organize a run-swim competition in Honolulu meant for endurance athletes who wanted something more than a marathon run. Shortly thereafter, during that same year, John thought of using a local cycling club route, completing the trifecta. The two looked at each other, and John famously said, "If you do it, I'll do it . . . whoever finishes first we'll call him the IRONMAN."

They proceeded to announce their newly created event at a local swim club banquet, and on February 18, 1978, the first-ever full-distance triathlon occurred. Word spread fast, and more and more people became interested in this remarkable test of endurance. ABC's *Wide World of Sports* broadcast the 1980 version of the event, sparking even more interest.

Growing in popularity over the years, it became nearly impossible to satisfy the hundreds of thousands of athletes who wanted to race in Kona, the biggest and best event each year. Kona is special. World Triathlon Corporation, owner of the IRONMAN brand, responded to event demand by creating a specific program to vet out applicants and choose who could participate in the IRONMAN World Championships in Kona. It decided that only the best of the best, from each age group, would qualify. And a few others.

Introduced in 2012, the lottery program made way for non-elite racers to have a chance to compete in the IRONMAN World Championship with the best and fastest in the sport. To qualify, you had to complete any full-distance triathlon sanctioned by the World Triathlon Corporation. Do that, and you could apply for a lottery spot. If chosen, you would find yourself at the start of the most anticipated and celebrated triathlons in one of the most challenging, beautiful, and historic places in the world.

Each year 2,500 people automatically qualify for the IRONMAN World Championship in Kona by being at the top of their age group, but the rest of us have to complete our races, send in our applications, and pray that we get chosen for one of the 100 coveted lottery spots. I had applied for one in 2012, 2013, and 2014, but I wasn't chosen. To complicate matters, in 2015, the program morphed into the IRONMAN Kona Legacy Program. This gave the organization a way to recognize the most loyal and dedicated athletes. They changed the lottery entrance requirements to allow in only those athletes with twelve full-distance finishes under their belts. Now, with the change in the selection process, I felt a renewed sense of hope that I could somehow secure a spot at Kona. I had completed nine races by 2016, including stops in Frankfurt, Germany; Whistler, British Columbia; and several others in the US.

By this point, and with only three more finishes left, I was within striking distance of the Legacy Lottery. My given Russian (now Ukrainian) name is Vichislav. One of my oldest friends stills calls me Vichy, a nickname that only she continues to use. When I learned of a newly announced IRONMAN Vichy, France, I just had to do it. In August of 2017, I flew out to Vichy with my older daughter. We had a great time in Paris before heading down to this spa and resort town for the race.

This race was unique in that the run course consisted of four 6.5-mile loops, with the end of each loop passing right next to the finishing chute. It was quite frustrating to see the faster runners fork right towards the finish line while the announcer bellowed out " . . . you are an IRONMAN." Of course, I had to fork left for another, then another, than yet another loop. Everything else about the venue was excellent and I had a decent finishing time of fourteen hours and nine minutes. Our hotel was about two miles away from the start/finish line though, which made for a painful walk home. Thankfully, Stephanie handled my bike and carried most of my gear. She fell asleep right as we arrived at the hotel, leaving me to disassemble and pack my bike and fight through my post-race cramps. To make matters worse, we had an early flight out of Paris the next day. Leaving the hotel before sunrise was a hard pill to swallow while desperate for sleep and trying to recover. Poor planning will hamper, if not ruin, any personal or professional endeavor.

I had two races left after Vichy. For my next race, I returned to IRONMAN Lake Placid in New York to re-experience this legendary venue. I built into the event another memorable weekend, this time with both my girls. For my final qualifying race in May of 2019, I chose the vineyards of Sonoma Valley for IRONMAN Santa Rosa. I took my younger daughter with me for this one. It's unfortunate this race was discontinued, as I really enjoyed the venue and vividly remember the chilly but beautiful reservoir swim. With the race being earlier in the season, I was a bit undertrained and really suffered on the run course. I finished just eighteen minutes before the seventeen-hour race cutoff time. Fortunately, my time was irrelevant, as finishing was all that mattered. After that race, it didn't take me long to put my application in for the Legacy Lottery, sending in that email just a few days after I crossed the finish line in California.

I waited and waited and waited, eagerly anticipating a response. One came just a couple of months later. I won't soon forget that feeling, as it seemed like all my hard work had paid off. I accomplished something few people had, and now, armed with twelve races under my belt, I could complete my dream and make it to the promised land. But there was a caveat. The IRONMAN World Championship had become extraordinarily popular, and while I punched my golden ticket, I was informed I would have to wait until October 2022 to race. A large applicant field forced World Triathlon Corporation to book some legacy athletes three years down the road.

To no one's surprise, it was also required to continue to race to maintain eligibility. It was a smart marketing scheme and kept us all signing up for their races. Luckily, they waived the need for a race in 2020, mostly due to COVID-19 event cancellations. That left 2021, and I had to complete one event to qualify. To be safe, I decided to sign up and compete in three full-distance triathlons, with the first two on back-to-back weekends. They were all stateside, one in Maryland, one in Wisconsin, and one in Florida as the final backup. Wisconsin came first, and I was geared up and ready to go. But for some reason, I bombed the bike ride and saw the worst words you could imagine: Did Not Finish (DNF). More on that later.

That was a true heartbreaker as it meant two things: First, I would have no choice but to race that second weekend because I really didn't want to wait a few more months for Florida. And, second, I would have to officially finish to qualify for the World Championships, or keep training and risk DNF'ing in Florida and then be bounced from Kona eligibility. I raced in Wisconsin on a Sunday, then flew back home to rest and recover for only a few days before driving to Maryland. My body didn't feel ready to turn around and compete again, but what choice did I have? One more 2.4-mile swim, 112-mile bike ride, and a 26.2-mile full-marathon run.

When I arrived in Maryland, I quickly recognized my mind, not my body, would carry the day. Still gasping for vital recovery time, my mind told my body to push through and get it done. Thankfully, that is exactly what happened. Somehow, someway, I made it to the finish line. This time I was much more confident when I started my "Kona, here I come!" chant to my wife, who was nervously awaiting my finish. She was always my biggest supporter. My time was actually one hour faster than the previous week and the finish was official, so I retained my eligibility and qualification for Kona. While I had been there before, it felt like the first time I had ever completed a race. Perhaps it was the pressure of having to finish, but it was such a gratifying feeling. Finally, for the first time, Kona seemed to be in reach. I made it. I qualified. And now, all I had to do was train.

The Legacy Lottery gave me something I never once thought I could achieve. When I started racing, there was no clear path to get to Kona other than qualify through placing at the top of my age group. This wasn't my life's work, and I was also working hard building a business. There just wasn't the luxury of putting everything else on the shelf just to train and race. Kona was always the eventual goal, but as I completed more and more triathlons, I began to understand and realize the reality of the IRONMAN World Championship. It was the promised land of sorts, and the only logical culmination of my dedication to the sport.

After returning home from Maryland, I felt relieved. While I didn't need Kona to justify my racing, it was certainly a dream. Like anything in life, you have to set reachable but significant goals. Then, as you move forward and accomplish more, it is only natural to continue to push the envelope and constantly adjust your goals and your target. That prevents you from being complacent and ambivalent. Perhaps the most amazing part of it all was that I felt so average, but I was seeking to achieve something so extraordinary. My journey to Kona started by getting off the couch and deciding to be more active, and it turned into a ten-plus-year journey that seemed to parallel my personal and professional growth.

Kona wasn't the only thing coming full circle in my life. In 2016, I decided to replace myself as CEO and step aside to become Executive Chairman. We hired Nick Wilkinson as Chief Operating Officer that same year, and quickly it became obvious that he was a remarkable addition to our team. My big idea was to leave Nick in that position for a year, ensure that I liked and trusted him and that he was the right fit to potentially lead my baby. Well, that lasted about three months. He was the perfect fit and quickly took over for me as CEO at the beginning of 2017. I felt that I had hit yet another lottery and with Nick in place, I could take a few steps away from Binary Tree and dig into my racing more than I ever had before.

It was an interesting time, as I recognized two things: Professionally, Nick could take the business much further than I could, and I would in turn receive better success while also receiving the gift to focus on my personal journey. It took a lot to run a business and a lot to train for triathlons, and yet some more to continue my mountaineering hobby. No way could I be fully effective at doing all three. It wasn't as if I reached a breaking point, but I was at a very important fork in the road. We've all been there, and thankfully I made the right choice for myself.

As 2019 concluded, I surveyed my life and felt pretty good about it. I had a new CEO and a new management team, and I recognized a great deal of personal and professional growth. Things seemed to be going in the right direction on all fronts. But there was also a lot of change. It was very different to see someone running my company, even if it was by choice. Nick was gracious about my initial hovering and opinions, knowing that I had just given him complete control over my baby. That was partly why I stepped aside in the first place. It is easy to allow emotion to creep in when you are so intimately connected to a situation.

Nick wasn't encumbered by the emotions that I had. He could see the forest for the trees and make extremely reasonable and objective decisions based on hard data. As I gave up control, he was empowered to do a fantastic job. We continued to meet at least once a week, spending time together discussing the company and its direction. This allowed me to feel involved, and it allowed Nick to consider my opinions since I knew the industry and our company better than anyone else.

Between passing the reins of my company and qualifying for the Legacy Lottery, it seemed like two very important parts of my life had come full circle. There was obviously a lot of work to do to get that coveted spot in the IRONMAN World Championship. When I found out I'd been chosen, I felt like I had hit my dream of racing in such a monumental event. Maybe just as important, at least to me, was that I would be forever tied to such a remarkable organization and successful endeavor. No one could take that away from me.

This wasn't the first time I had felt that way. When IBM selected Binary Tree as a trusted partner, I felt the same exact way. We tied our success to their bandwagon, and it brought immediate accolades and respect. The same was true when I raced Kona. They chose me, and everyone knew it. Later on, in my professional life, we left IBM and partnered with Microsoft, another juggernaut of the industry. Same outcome—immediate credibility.

Whether I realized it at the time or not, we had found our niche in the ecosystem of the industry as a small but vital symbiotic partner to the big guys—the pilot fish to their shark—making the most of our collaborative efforts. We had built a very large and successful company, at least in part, based on our partnerships and the good will they created. In many ways, we are a product of the relationships and groups and individuals with which we run, bike, or swim.

Now, I had no intention to rest on my accomplishments, but I felt like I had found a great deal of balance in two of the most important areas of my life. The harder you work, the luckier you get. This was one of the key mantras during this part of my life. Sure, I was doing the work—training my ass off, putting in long hours at the office, and doing everything I could to scale our business while building strong relationships. But it still took a few lucky breaks to get closer and closer to the goals I had set.

For starters, I was lucky to have picked two races back to back and a third as additional backup in 2021. I was unlucky to have not finished one of them, but at least I had a second or even a third chance to qualify if needed. World Triathlon Corporation selected my legacy lottery application, which left me feeling particularly fortunate. Had I not finished those twelve races, though, I wouldn't have had a chance. On the business front, I was lucky to have found a successor and fortunate for all the positive developments we saw in our industry and for our company. With Microsoft's success in the cloud, there was an increased need for our products and services, and that offered more and more opportunity to succeed. For example, Hewlett Packard selected Binary Tree as its go-to vendor for email migration, and that furthered our position in the marketplace. That "luck" didn't occur overnight. It took years and years of hard work and dedication to build our brand and reputation so that a company like HP would recognize and choose us over other industry players.

Sure, luck played a role. It impacts each of our lives. Our new CEO, Nick, could have punched his card at any tech company in the country. He was a great guy, well respected and liked, and extremely knowledgeable. Nick chose Binary Tree, I came to learn, because of our culture and energy. He felt connected to us and decided my humble little company would be the best place to take the next step in his career. That was luck. But I built that over ten years of rebuilding and making good hiring decisions to create a team that people wanted to join. We had great products, a strong trajectory, and very low employee turnover. Nick was smart enough to recognize that.

To some degree, there really is no luck. No bad luck. No good luck. Just decisions.

Just outcomes. Just breaks. Just opportunity. It is how you, the one who controls your fate, chooses to respond to your circumstances that dictates the ultimate resolution. It is easy to blame luck when things go wrong—"I just got unlucky." In doing so, however, you forego a learning opportunity. You take a chance to figure out why you got unlucky and potentially improve and trade it for the complacency of just assuming things happen the way they happen without explanation. They don't.

There are lessons to be learned in the good outcomes, the bad outcomes, and the neutral ones.

A lottery is a funny thing. The very definition of it is that it is an outcome governed by chance. Sure, chance plays a role in most situations, but you have to constantly ask yourself this: What can I do to reduce the uncontrollable aspect of chance? Once we all start working to reduce it, we can begin to shift our behaviors to move in the direction of securing what we really care about—the greatest possible outcome.

The Legacy Lottery, an outcome that is supposed to be completely governed by chance, chose me. The guy who put in the work. Who scheduled back-to-back races and one more for safety to ensure he didn't slip and tried to guarantee himself a second and third chance if he did. Is that chance? Is that luck? Or, as I would like to think of it, maybe it's just destiny.

Key Takeaways

- Be thoughtful about your choice of running partners in life and business. A good fit can take you a long way.

- Always have contingency plans and be ready to execute them when things don't go your way.

- You make your own luck through hard work and good decisions.

AVOIDING THE BONK

ARMED WITH ADMISSION via the Legacy Lottery and an opportunity to race in the IRONMAN World Championship in Kona, Hawaii, I was elated. It seemed like I had finally reached the Promised Land, ten years in the making. I had started this humble journey years and years before receiving that fateful email, and it was a monumental occasion I was lucky enough to share with my family. But, as I learned quickly, I still had a lot of work to do before putting my feet on the volcanic ground. Amazingly enough, as I write this chapter, I am less than twenty-four hours away from boarding a flight to Hawaii and finally experiencing the most amazing triathlon journey of them all.

Racing triathlons has taught me a lot about myself, my life, and the world in general—the highs, the lows, and the everything-in-between. There are a lot of these lessons, but perhaps one of the greatest of them all is a lesson in falling short, a warning of failure. Or, as we say on the racecourse, "Avoid the bonk."

You see, it is quite common for one to fail in a triathlon—to swim, bike, and run hard, but even so, not make it to the finish line. Athletes time out, burn out, or as some call it, *bonk*. *Bonk* refers to when your body runs out of glucose to burn, and your muscles and liver are then depleted of glycogen. Because glycogen is the primary fuel source for your brain, bonking can make you experience central nervous system fatigue as well.

We have all been there, experiencing that feeling of total body exhaustion, as if we have completely run out of gas. It is a concerning feeling, and low blood sugar can impact our basic anatomy to the extent that we cannot function. The dreaded bonk can come on quick, and it is remarkably hard to recover from. On most occasions, racers experience the bonk because they fail to use their resources wisely.

Like nearly anything in the human body, glucose is a scarce and finite resource. The more we use it, the more we must put back in. Normally, that is an easy task. But when you are racing a triathlon, it is easy to lose track of your resources and energy levels, which leads to the bonk. Let me tell you, it is too late to do much of anything once you hit that bonk. In some ways, it is unrecoverable. Full system failure.

With over a dozen full-distance triathlons under my belt, I have fought that feeling and experience of going out too fast. For me, it often happens on the swim. The swim is the first discipline in the race and often seems to be the most chaotic. Over one thousand people race into the water, which is often turbulent to begin with, and start flailing their bodies, often kicking and hitting one another. It is pure chaos. Even as the pack begins to calm, you want to create separation. There are only two ways to do that: Get ahead or fall behind. I am sure you know which is preferred.

Ideally, it would be wonderful to slowly get acclimated to the water, dip your toes in, and then go on a light swim. Instead, you get to enjoy what feels like praying for survival in a human washing machine. You get incredibly winded, sometimes to the point of hyperventilating, and begin to look around for the nearby kayaks or rescue boats just in case you go under. It is the worst feeling in the world. It's not just the notion of failing. Rather, it is the feeling that you might not make it out of the swim alive.

In response, your body goes into fight-or-flight mode. You begin to gobble up valuable energy, wind, and glucose, so much so that your mind becomes deprived of the essential elements it needs to function. It's all a downhill slide from there. It's not nearly as dramatic, but it can happen on the bike or the run as well. Too fast a pace will eventually lead you to hit the wall and desperately search for unavailable resources. The bonk is your worst enemy. Often, it is directly tied to your nutrition or preparation for the race. Did you put enough resources into your body before you started the journey to carry you along the way? We ask ourselves that question over and over during the race.

The bonk is horrific, physically and mentally. As your body begins to fail, your mind often tries to push ahead. But the bonk even preys on your mental fortitude. Once those receptors stop firing, and the brain can't feed, it is just moments from full system failure. It takes time to build up to the bonk as you deplete precious resources. But it only takes minutes to watch it all fall apart. The full-body onslaught and attack is aggressive. Perhaps what makes it even worse is that we all know the bonk is avoidable.

The bonk isn't just a term reserved for triathlons. I see it and feel it all the time. When it comes to your personal or professional life, you may know it as burnout, that feeling that you have lost the ability to remain focused, engaged, and interested in what you are doing.

Sadly, burnout is one of the most common experiences in our fast-paced society. We often train ourselves to think that it is acceptable to work well past the reasonable boundaries of human existence. If you don't work until you can work no longer, then you clearly aren't giving it your best effort. I see it in the workplace all the time. On most occasions, it is a function of the work environment, demanding unreasonable amounts from employees and team members. Then, as is almost always the case, the team can't deliver. Team members are exhausted from trying, and the work suffers significantly.

When building Binary Tree, we did our best to create a culture of balance, one where people surely did work hard but were not facing totally unmanageable expectations. I wanted happy and energetic team members. I knew I had to keep their proverbial gas tanks filled to ensure they were ready to do the job and get us to the finish line. That calls for preparation and balance, really the cure for the bonk. Easy to say, hard to actually do. As a society, we often find ourselves lost in our work, pushing ourselves in a way that it is neither healthy nor a recipe for any type of reasonable lifestyle. Then, when the shit hits the fan, we are shocked. It is unfathomable to us that our bodies and minds couldn't sustain us as we went 100 percent full speed ahead.

The brick walls are always waiting for us, as nothing can possibly last forever. That is why balance is so important. It allows you to sustain a strong race for a longer time. Just think about it like a marathon . . . do you want to go fast for half of the race, and then bonk, or sustain a healthy pace for the entire race and get to the finish line? I know you agree with me that the key is to finish, not to run half at full speed. But be that as it may, we often still push ourselves and our bodies way past the point of reason. We know the right thing to do, but we helplessly do the opposite. Call it human nature or recognize that we allow external factors to influence us to make decisions we would not otherwise normally make.

You don't have to bonk. It is completely avoidable. To avoid the bonk, I do three things before and multiple times during a race:

1. **Full system check:** I survey my body and mind. I determine what hurts, what feels good, and what might need some extra attention. Being in tune with the physical aspects of your body can cause you to put energy and attention where it's needed. Far too many times, we don't take a few minutes to listen to our bodies, to recognize what we need and then to respond accordingly. Rather, we charge ahead with reckless abandonment and then seem fully shocked when everything falls apart. Your body is a high-performing machine. High-performing machines need to be tuned up and cared for.

2. **Stick to the plan:** The easiest and most obvious way to bonk is to lack proper preparation and plan execution of the race. Sometimes, we get so comfortable with the upcoming adventure that we forget to properly prepare for it and/or execute correctly during it. We know what to expect and assume nothing will go wrong. However, preparation and planning is a key component to successfully completing anything that really matters. Before each and every race, I survey my resources and those available to me on the racecourse and plan for their use. For example, each event has aid stations offering participants food and fluids. Before the race, I determine what they offer, look up the nutritional info and the brand names, and then supplement what I am carrying to match what I need above and beyond the resources I will get along the way. This simple step ensures I will have the sustenance necessary to complete the long road ahead.

3. **Balance my body and my mind:** This is probably the hardest thing to do, but you must find balance to ensure you reserve enough resources to get to the finish line. Just like you completed a full system check before the race, now you have to constantly check in with your body to determine how you are doing during

the race. Feeling a strain in your calf? A twinge in your hamstring? Thirsty? Lethargic? Blister forming? Remedy each of these issues before they cause you irreparable harm. Stop and stretch. Drink some water. Take a nutrition gel. Balance is key to completing anything that matters.

In the business world, you often read how the vast majority of businesses fail. The most important things to do to avoid your business from going in the wrong direction include the following:

1. **Monitoring your cash flow** maniacally and having more credit available to you then you'll ever need.

2. **Surrounding yourself with smart people** that have been there and done that. Hire executives and leaders not for your business's current level but for its next level (or two).

3. **Knowing all your numbers.** Define and track all the important KPI's and make sure all your leaders are doing the same.

In your personal life, burnout can also be avoided. My highest priorities for this have always been:

1. **Leading a balanced life.** I sure have put in my fair share of crazy hours that left little time for much else, but I sure tried hard to slip in #2 and #3 below. Hobbies have also been incredibly important to me so that I had something to look forward to outside of work. Reading (and learning), motorcycle riding, going to the beach, vacations, unique restaurants, skiing, scuba diving, and movies are just some of things I would always look forward to and still do in addition to my endurance sports addiction.

2. **Surrounding myself with people I'm happy to be around.** There will always be people that just refuse to be happy and won't hesitate to take up all your time together letting you know why and usually blame others for their condition. Or they can be plain old jerks. This happens at work and in one's personal life. Sometimes it's impossible to completely eliminate these kinds of people from your life, but you can try and control the conversation to be more favorable. Sometimes, certain relationships just need to end.

3. **Having as much fun and laughing as much as humanly possible.** No explanation needed. Be selfish when you have to. I am at times. It's medically proven that fun and laughter will add years to your life. Who wouldn't want a few extra?

No one wants to experience the bonk. Even so, and knowing just how real it is, we all find ourselves in a position of exhaustion or failure at times. That is part of life. What does not need to be part of your life, however, is experiencing the bonk on a regular basis. It happens now and again, but recognize the remarkable control you have over your ability to gauge your body, navigate challenging situations, and avoid hitting the wall before it's too late.

While not always easy, know yourself, your body, your mind, and, of course, your limitations. Your body speaks to you in a variety of ways. Learning how to listen to it is a gift that will serve you through any endeavor, big or small. Michael Jordan said, "I have failed many times, but I have never gone into a game expecting myself to fail." That is why the bonk is so dangerous—it is unexpected. If you knew it would have occurred, likely you would have changed your approach. It creeps up on you, and when it hits, it is too late to do anything but survive. At some point, your body can do no more and must look elsewhere for help. Thankfully, help is on the way.

Key Takeaways

- Whether you call it *bonk* or *burnout*, avoid pushing yourself past the point where you can function well.

- An exhausted team cannot deliver, no matter how hard they try.

- Preparation and balance are the cure to the bonk.

- The three steps to avoiding the bonk while racing are: full system check, prepare for the journey, and balance both body and mind.

- The three steps to avoiding the bonk in business are: monitor cash flow and credit, surround yourself with seasoned pros, and know your numbers.

- The three steps to avoiding the bonk in life are: lead a balanced life, pick who you surround yourself with, and laugh as much possible.

A RUNNER'S HIGH

WE'VE ALL EXPERIENCED IT—that euphoric moment where everything just feels right. Even perfect. It is the zone. The flow. The remarkable instance when everything else fades away and you are totally engaged in exactly what you are doing. A runner's high is pure elation, overwhelmingly perfect, and something that we all chase. Before I started extensively training for races and competing in them, I didn't fully understand, nor had I experienced a runner's high. But once I did, I knew I wanted more.

When racing triathlons and ascending mountains, you push your mind and body to the absolute limit. You often go much farther than you ever thought you could. In doing so, you may feel like you can travel no longer, and quitting seems like the only available option. That is when the runner's high kicks in. It's an instinctual response to your body saying, "No more." It's almost like a relief of sorts, a break for the mind and the body. You know exactly when you start to flow and get in the zone.

In short, it is special. Frankly, as any runner may tell you, it is an amazing feeling that helps you get through the fatigue, the pain, and the suffering. Your body wants to throw in the white flag, but your brain grabs it before it hits the ground and leads the charge to keep going. I have competed in many races, and that feeling of euphoria appears around the same time in each race. Usually, after one mile during the swim, on mile fifty of the bike, and mile seven on the run, when I am feeling down and out, I start to get this sense of pure jubilation.

No longer focused on the lethargy in my mind or the sting in my joints, everything seems to come together and fire at once, like a finely tuned machine doing its job. It is the sense that you and your body are giving 100 percent effort, the sweet spot of purity that keeps it all going at once. You don't have to experience the runner's high to know exactly what I'm talking about. We see it occur on the basketball court or football field all the time. The jump shooter who can't miss, or the quarterback who completes ten passes in a row. In terms of individual sports, like golf or tennis, it is the athlete who hits on every shot, knocks in each long putt, or is totally unflappable. In yoga we call it *flow*, where you seem to transition from one position to the next without effort or energy loss.

But this feeling of bliss is not limited to sports. When writing, there might be long periods where the words simply flow out of your mind and onto the paper. Now, that didn't happen to me when I wrote this book, but I kept my head down and battled through. Or perhaps you are working on a client's project, and your team continues to produce better and better ideas. Maybe you are an artist creating a perfect masterpiece with every stroke of the brush. There really is no better feeling of productivity and sense of purpose.

I remember many times at Binary Tree when a herculean effort was needed to win a large project. Then even before the ink was dry on the signed contract another large opportunity would present itself. High off the previous closed deal, we would jump right in and get to work on the next one. Just like surfing waves come in sets, often so would large deals.

The point is that, no matter what you do, especially when it comes to your business, it is crucial that you find that peacefulness in your work. It is really a combination of finding something you love that utilizes your gifts. If you do that, it is quite likely you will feel purposeful and recognize amazing results.

When I first experienced the runner's high, I didn't quite realize what it was. In fact, I wasn't sure I even liked the feeling; it seemed too good to be true, fully connecting me with my core while disconnecting me from the pain I expected my body to continue to experience. But as it took over and I surrendered to it, a magical thing happened. I could keep going in perfect harmony. It occurred in one of my first marathons and then in a triathlon, and since then, it seems like an angel on my shoulder that appears when I need it the most.

This has been most beneficial during ultramarathons. Technically, an ultramarathon is any running race which covers a distance greater than a regular marathon of 26.2 miles. The most popular versions include 50k, 50 miles, 100k, and 100 miles. There are also some extreme versions with even longer distances. I've completed several of these, and boy does a runner's high come in handy when you're out there on your feet from sunrise to often way past sunset.

I've completed the following ultramarathons: Monument Valley 50k in Colorado, Border to Badlands 50k in Texas, and the Zion 50k in Utah. I liked Zion so much that I returned in 2022 to run the 100k there. It is hard to explain the phenomenon of going from being ready to throw in the towel to all of a sudden feeling like you've just started with all the energy in the world. My wife's response to my 3 a.m. call asking for a pickup from the finish line is something she'd rather not explain either.

A runner's high, flow, being in the zone, is often a product of the circumstances around you. Specifically, as it relates to the runner's high, it is imperative that you are in a moment of great exertion. It is almost like your mind's response to extreme conditions. Your brain recognizes that your body is in need of assistance and kicks in with a hard reset to help you continue. It is a tremendous response and demonstrates the true power of mind over body.

Back to my previous example, a break from burning the midnight oil might sound like just what the doctor ordered, but experiencing the results of our efforts gave us the high to rinse and repeat again and again.

We all have physical limitations. Perhaps we can't jump as high or run as fast as we once did. Maybe we lost that explosiveness on the basketball court or the ability to throw a baseball fifty yards with the flick of a wrist. Physical attributes fade. But your mind is your strongest muscle, and it fades at a much slower rate than your body. In fact, if you exercise it daily, your mind will get stronger, more robust, more capable. It is truly amazing how it can evolve and accomplish more and more and more.

So, it should be no surprise just how important it is to rely on your mind in times of great need and stress. Whether you realize it, your mind is the captain of the ship. It makes every single piece work. It sends the signals to each of your muscles to fire, to move, to rest, and to work. Buddha said, "Your mind is everything. What you think, you become." It is completely limitless, supporting you in all your endeavors, whether they be easy or complicated. Like Henry Ford said, "Whether you think you can, or you think you can't—you're right."

Competing in long-distance endurance events, the kind that take hours or even days, can be remarkably emotional. Most anything of merit and worth takes time. There is no instant finish line. You have to put in the work to get there. I call it "the reach," but it's really that time when you have to extend past what you believe you are capable of to push through and get to where you need to go. We've all been there before. You may just be inches away from your goals, but in the moment, it feels like you are miles away. You have to battle through those moments, reach just a little more, and grab onto your goals. It's just one example, but the physiological response that is the runner's high helps you reach farther than imaginable and get to the finish line.

We were once going against our largest competitor for a seven-figure deal. While it looked promising at first, the potential client went silent on us. They stopped returning emails and voicemails, but we continued to try and re-engage for months. After nine months our lead account executive told me she was taking the deal out of her pipeline because she felt it was lost. I asked her if the potential client had asked to stop being contacted and she said they had not. I reminded her of my favorite outbound sales belief. You never stop calling/emailing until you are asked to do so. I joined the effort, and we tag teamed them with emails and phone calls. We won that deal three months later.

I still recall a particularly difficult race in Frankfurt, Germany. I had recently lost my father and my uncle, who were both coincidentally named Alex. It was an emotional time, and I was looking forward to the break a race would offer. However, leading up to race day, I made several rookie mistakes. I spent the day before in the sun, had a few German beers, and didn't get a good night's rest. There is no other way to say it: I was completely off.

From the beginning, I realized that it wasn't going to be easy. I started crashing very quickly, and the hot summer sun was just pounding on me. During the run portion as I was beginning to get nervous, unsure if I was going to make it, a strange sense of spirituality overtook me. Then, as that seemed to be at the height of its influence on me, I felt a much-welcomed runner's high come on. I felt like I could push through, and I looked down at the ground. Then, I saw the word "Alex" on three occasions. It looked as if someone had etched the name into the concrete.

Now, it is not abnormal for spectators to write things in chalk on the race grounds to show love and support for the participants, but this seemed eerily strange. I was there by myself as no family members could make the international trip. So, it is fair to say that no one actually wrote the name "Alex" on the ground for me. I was either completely hallucinating or it was a remarkable coincidence. Nonetheless, I still, to this day, feel like a higher being and force helped me fight through my exhaustion and complete the race.

A runner's high can feel like an altered state of mind. Perhaps that is why we use the word *high*, which is the very act of inducing an altered state through the introduction of a foreign substance. But the best kind of high is the natural one. You can't always simulate it or produce it on a whim, but when it comes, it is pure elation and joy. Thus, I can tell you that we all can craft a mindset that supports our brain function and invites the reciprocity of support a healthy mind can offer. As Kemi Sogunle says, "What you feed your mind, will lead your life."

My business high came in many forms, but my favorite was trade shows. They were the collection of thousands of customers and hundreds of us vendors in one large venue. The hustle and bustle of these events was a great reminder of how much opportunity there was out there. We always left with new relationships, new ideas, and new opportunities to pursue.

Trade shows were also used as an opportunity to reunite in person with employees from around the country and the world. We would often bookend these events with internal meetings with attending staff. It was a great opportunity to continue to build our corporate culture, get feedback from the field in person, and rally the troops around our goals and objectives.

I would always return back to the office reinvigorated with the energy and positivity to continue to go after it.

I have over 10,000 miles worth of endurance races and training to tell you that the more positivity I invite into my mind, the greater the chance it will help me when I am in need. A healthy mind supports a healthy body, and just like we don't feed our bodies crap and expect full productivity, we can't feed our minds negative thoughts and expect they will fire on all cylinders.

As I see it, we are all empowered to decide to be the best versions of ourselves; to demonstrate great discipline, determination, and, of course, effort. It isn't always easy to shut off the noise and focus on the task at hand, but the more we can devote 100 percent of our bodies and minds to our goals and dreams, the better chance we will have to reach them. The brain is a remarkable muscle. It cares for us and ensures we are headed in the right direction. It course corrects when we need it the most. And, as you can see in this chapter, it pushes us further than we could ever go on our own. As Leon Brown said, "It all begins and ends in your mind. What you give power to, has power over you, if you allow it." Choose wisely, as that decision will inevitably control your destiny.

Key Takeaways

- Your mind is powerful. Let positivity carry you through tough times.

- Invite positivity in as often as you can. The more you do, the more stores you have to draw upon when you need to.

- Always exercise your mind.

15

ENVISION THE FINISH

IT FEELS AMAZING to break through the wall and find a renewed sense of ability and energy to reach goals. However, that goal, the finish line, may still be a ways down the road. That may mean there is work to be done before you complete the cycle and accomplish what you set out to do. For both my business and my endurance racing and adventure career, I have made a habit of setting lofty goals and striving to achieve them. They aren't always easy, especially when they are still years (or many miles) away. That is part of goal setting, though: choosing specific ambitions or objects that are big enough to matter. These are the ones we rarely manifest overnight. They take a great deal of patience—sometimes more than we think we are capable of. That is why it is crucial to learn how to maintain a strong vision for these goals and constantly imagine the finish line, even though you might not otherwise be able to see it.

When you learn how to envision your goals, the victory is always near. You can feel it, almost as if it is deeply planted in your existence. It stays with you and acts as a subtle reminder to continue forward, maintain your drive, and never, ever give up. I have been envisioning my goals since the beginning of Binary Tree, dating back to my first sales meetings. Before walking into a meeting, and specifically the oversized skyscraper in which it was housed, I would stop at the doorstep, close my eyes, and imagine the meeting.

I imagined each and every detail, from the feeling of walking into the room, shaking the hands of the prospective clients, taking my seat, and beginning to deliver my PowerPoint presentation. I envisioned the key speaking points, making eye contact with each attendee, and, of course, the close. Then, in those final fateful seconds before walking into the building, I foresaw and visualized closing the deal and signing up another client. It was and still is a remarkable and powerful exercise, and whether or not I end up successfully closing the client, I feel energized and in the right mindset to give the pitch my best effort.

Now, this ability to visualize and manifest an outcome didn't happen overnight. It is a muscle I have developed, and I continue to work it out again and again. Even today, I find myself practicing visualization often, knowing the better I am at doing it, the higher the likelihood I will be successful in my endeavors. As I write this chapter, I just recently completed the IRONMAN World Championship in Kona. When I first decided to explore this tremendous goal, I printed out a picture of the banner for the event. Then, I taped it onto a wall near my computer so I could face that goal each and every day.

The banner acted as a huge motivator and kept me focused and dedicated to what seemed like a lofty and distant goal. I would often find myself daydreaming as I looked at the oversized wording and the backdrop of the beautiful Hawaiian terrain. During my training, and competing in triathlon after triathlon, you can imagine there were plenty of days I didn't want to suit up and go for a long run or a swim at the local gym. But that simple yet effective picture brought me back, grounded me, and reminded me why I was doing what I was doing. Seeing the goal allowed me to envision it time and time again.

I cannot overstate the remarkable value of envisioning your goals. Whether they are financial, relationship oriented, health focused, professionally grounded, or nearly anything else of meaning, visualizing your goals carries remarkable significance and benefit. Perhaps the best thing about visualization is just how easy and cost effective it is. By that I mean that it only takes a few minutes each day or week. It costs nothing and allows you to work the most valuable muscle you have, your brain. As you visualize more and more, your body begins to fully buy into the vision your mind is creating and propels you toward your goal.

In another time, it sounded unbelievable to think I could sell my business. It was even more of a reach to consider selling it for a life-changing amount of money. Even so, that was my goal. I wasn't always sure how I could reach it, but I felt confident that working hard every single day would be part of the impetus to get there. As we built Binary Tree into a successful industry leader, this big dream began to look more and more like a reality, so much so that I started to visualize an executive from a large business handing over a check to purchase my company. I imagined what that check might look like, and, of course, the amount on it. I visualized every last detail, even going so far as to imagine how I might feel when I received it, fulfilling my greatest dream.

In many ways, I put myself in the room, and I could feel and see this special moment. I trained my mind to welcome in the opportunity and remain motivated to forge ahead toward this dream. This simple act made it seem attainable, and I loved the idea of accomplishing such a remarkable goal. Eventually, I did sell my company. It was a special moment, one I felt like I had lived through again and again. Déjà vu of sorts, I had been there before. It didn't feel new or unfamiliar. Rather, it seemed like I had sold my company dozens of times over. This is the true power of visualization. It is not in just getting there. It is in understanding how you will feel or react when you arrive.

Great basketball players visualize knocking down two free throws to win the big game. NFL and collegiate placekickers imagine kicking the ball through the uprights to win a game in overtime. Baseball players envision a swing of the bat that brings the runners on loaded bases home for the win. Actors rehearse their lines ad nauseam. Why do they do this? So, when they have to perform under pressure, they have a sense of belonging and familiarity with an otherwise pressure-inducing situation.

Visualization isn't necessarily a skill that you are born with. Rather, it is something we can all develop with careful and pointed training and repetition. At first it might feel kind of strange to visualize something that might not even happen. But the more you do it, the more likely it is to happen. It takes on a life of its own and begins to feel real. This offers you the inspiration and motivation you might not otherwise have to continue working toward your goals and your dreams.

It might take some trial and error on your behalf. You manifest, and it works. You manifest, and fall short. What was the difference? Were you doing it every single day? Did you truly buy into the process? Were you focused when you visualized your goals? Did you eliminate all other influences? Manifesting is hardly an overwhelming practice, but it does require discipline and dedication. Through the sheer power of your brain, you arm yourself with the ability to influence your subconscious behavior and lead yourself down new paths of opportunity.

Start with just a few minutes alone with your thoughts. Then, as you master that practice, begin to write down your goals. Find a handy notebook and constantly journal your dreams, being very specific about what they look and feel like. Choose pictures from the internet or from magazines and put them in common areas of your house or office. The repetitious review of these goals develops muscle memory in your brain, and you can tap into that reservoir daily to perpetuate your goals. It is truly an undeniable and powerful resource.

When I first embarked on the somewhat overwhelming task of writing a book, I hired a graphic designer to proactively design the cover art. I didn't even have a publisher or a marketing plan. But I knew if I looked at that cover a few times a day, I would remain steadfast in my dedication to bring this project along, making it a priority and getting to the finish line without question. As I write these very words, that draft cover remains near my computer, and I often look at it to stay dedicated to the ultimate goal.

While I have achieved many of my goals, I still covet climbing to the top of Denali, the highest mountain peak in North America. It's a lofty goal, especially since two prior attempts were unsuccessful; but I know I will reach the summit one day. In fact, walk into my office and you will see various pictures of the top of this monster of a mountain. If I am being honest, I have had these pictures hanging around for far too long, as this goal has percolated in my mind, even though I have summited its taller cousin Mount Aconcagua in South America. I continue to visualize successfully summiting Denali often, and this dream will eventually become a reality. I already know which mountain pic is going up next after I achieve this goal.

What about you? Pause, and think about it. What are some of your biggest goals and aspirations? Run a marathon? Get a master's degree?

Receive a raise or promotion? Find a husband or wife? Enhance your relationship with God? Have children? Buy a bigger house? These are all larger-than-life goals. But they don't have to be. You can choose to visualize even smaller and more attainable ones. Get in better shape? Spend less money on wasteful purchases? Read a book each month? Spend less time on social media? That is the true beauty of visualization. Big or small, it can impact your life in remarkable ways. No goal or dream is too big or small, and the practice for reading a new book each month is exactly the same as writing one.

Sometimes, though, it can be helpful to take larger goals and break them down into more attainable chunks. I do that all the time. When first I decided to compete in full-distance triathlons, I didn't immediately race the full length. Rather, I chose to run a half-marathon first. Then a full marathon. Then I added in a swim. Then a longer swim. I cycled and eventually went on longer and longer bike rides. You see, it is crucial to build on your goals but to do so one step at a time. Otherwise, reaching your goals can be difficult if not impossible to achieve.

Think about what it would take to create a new product. First, you must come up with the concept. Then, you must begin to build it. Next, you have to take your prototypes and test their quality. Likely, you'll have to make adjustments after that step. Ready to bring it to market? Don't forget about packaging. Consider how you will market the product. What will it cost to ship it? How will you sell it? Who is your ideal consumer? These are all crucial questions. The more you break these considerations down into smaller and more bite-sized chunks, the better. This allows you to fully focus on each individual piece of the process, forcing you to truly consider how to best succeed and not overlook any part of the journey. Visualizing each step will also better position you to recognize where you are set and ready to go and where you need extra help. It will work to highlight blind spots and allow you to adjust before the race begins.

Despite the fact that the finish line is often a very specific target, sometimes no finish line to speak of exists. We come across those often. There is no finish line in life. Of course, death may seem like a logical conclusion, but I don't want you visualizing the end. Rather, visualize how you want to live each day. What steps can you take to live a purposeful and meaningful life? How can you take full advantage of each blessing bestowed upon you? Now, this isn't easy. Often, we waste so much time and energy on things that don't matter at the cost of so much opportunity. Then, looking back, we wonder where all the time went.

Life is precious. Moments are fleeting. Time has a way of escaping us. But when we become extremely aware and considerate of our limited time, we can devote much more concentrated effort to what really matters. Stay the course and do your best to envision everything that matters to you. Remember the three steps that will carry you through this process:

1. Break down larger goals into smaller goals.

2. Devote yourself to visualizing each day.

3. Execute on your visualization through concerted action.

These simple yet powerful guiding principles will help you win the day. They will give you hope and help dreams become reality. I have witnessed the power of this again and again. In fact, I devote time each day to imagining what I want in the future. Put yourself at the finish line from the moment you start the journey, and you will find that your mind and body will feel inspired and motivated to navigate the road ahead.

Key Takeaways

- When you learn how to envision your goals, the victory is always near.

- Identify your biggest goals and aspirations.

- Take larger goals and break them down into more attainable chunks.

- Visualize how you want to live each day.

16

THE IMPORTANCE
OF ELASTIC LACES

THERE IS A LOT to racing triathlons and summiting a mountain. Like nearly anything in life that is worth a damn, your overall success is often a product of external factors, like the terrain and the weather, and internal factors, like your training, diet, and gear. When I first started racing, I was just happy to be there. Getting to the finish line was my sole focus. I hardly cared when or how I got there. I just wanted to finish. Nothing more, nothing less. But as I began racing more and more, I soon realized a certain level of competition with not just the other racers but with myself. In response, I began to place a priority on finding each and every single advantage, big or small. Unaware of what might be available to me, there were plenty of small things I could do to gain several advantages. These smaller advantages would often have larger benefits, making the race easier to complete, shaving valuable seconds or minutes off of my time, and even helping me make the cutoff.

One such advantage most triathletes enjoy is elastic laces. In their simplest form, elastic laces are a substitute for traditional shoelaces, allowing you to just throw on your running shoes as you transition from the bike to the run. They turn any pair of sneakers into literal slip-ons, where you can just slide your feet in and hit the roadway, losing little time in moving from one discipline to another. While spending thirty seconds tying your shoes may not seem like the end of the world to you, just ask how important that can be to the thousands of racers who missed their personal record or worse, the cutoff, by twenty seconds.

Competing in triathlon is hard enough, and there is tremendous value in finding every advantage you can. The more you compete in these races, the more you'll realize how each one seems to be neck and neck. The pack eventually thins out, but rarely are you swimming, biking, or running without other competitors nearby. In fact, the difference between first and fourth, the difference in medaling or not, is often just a few seconds. Think about watching an Olympic sport. How many times is the winner just an arm's length ahead of the pack? Most times, right?

When competing against great athletes, the disparity is razor thin. Triathletes spend a fortune on their bikes because they choose to purchase the lightest but strongest performing piece of equipment available on the market. The less they have to pull across the lengthy course, the better. There is a benefit to less weight. Because triathlons are so lengthy and involved, many opportunities exist to shave time and reduce your expenditure. That is the value of elastic laces.

For me, discovering these hidden gimmicks became one of the most exciting parts of race preparation. I always love, in work or on the course, finding ways to perform at a higher level. These small adjustments can deliver significant results. Some refer to this concept as incremental improvement, and I agree that little shifts, changes, and alterations can turn into performance-changing results. In everything that we do, including but not limited to racing, opportunities exist to improve our performance.

As we built Binary Tree into a scalable and successful business, we often used the idea of elasticity throughout our business decisions. I mean that we did two things: First, we were always flexible. Just like an elastic band that can stretch great distances and return back to form, we always remained willing to pursue stretch goals and get out of our comfort zone. The second aspect of this concept: We were always looking at ways to incrementally improve. Recognizing that we weren't going to change overnight, I became somewhat obsessed with determining the best adjustments I could make for our team to increase the likelihood of reaching goals.

That often meant taking a significant look at product development, professional services, account executives, managers, solution architects, inside sales, and, of course, outsourcing versus keeping things in-house. There was so much room to grow and evolve in each of these areas, and even saving a little bit of time or money on each step in the process could turn into millions of dollars of increased revenue or tremendous time-saving efforts.

Learning about elastic laces not only saved me time on the racecourse, but it also opened my eyes to how something so simple could benefit me. Elasticity makes me think of stretching. Early in my racing career, I didn't quite realize the importance of stretching. Of course, I knew it existed, but I just didn't give it much weight. But when I started racing seriously, I realized just how crucial stretching would be to my overall success.

Stretching, or manipulating and expanding your muscles, not only warms you up to prepare you for the race, but it also helps you recover.

It also prepares your muscles to be pushed, manipulated, and controlled in various ways. Stretching can condition your body to better respond to fatigue and difficult challenges. I'm a yoga enthusiast. According to the National Institutes of Health, scientific evidence shows that yoga supports stress management, mental health, mindfulness, healthy eating, weight loss, and sleep quality. It can also improve your strength, balance, and flexibility. It can help your heart and ease arthritis symptoms. Sounds pretty good, right? Just think about that for a second. Yoga, grounded in stretching and manipulating your body to expand the muscles, carries the many benefits just outlined.

Being elastic, or flexible, can make a difference not just to your race time but also to your business, your personal health, and to your relationships. Elasticity allows something to return to its normal shape spontaneously after contraction, dilation, or distortion. Just think about how that might help you in your life. So many obstacles or challenges stretch us, causing us to distort and dilate. It happens to us often. When they strike, it is quite common to respond with stress, anxiety, and frustration. That's because they take us out of our comfort zone, remove us from what is familiar, and thrust us into difficult scenarios.

If we were elastic like those shoelaces, no matter how hard something tugged at us we could easily return back to our normal form. That would be amazing. Truly life changing. Well, I am here to tell you that we are elastic and capable of stretching and returning back to our basic form. It becomes a mindset shift, recognizing what we can do to stretch ourselves without losing our true form. We can face challenges, overcome them, and do so without feeling like they will break us.

It is truly remarkable what you can learn about yourself and the world around you by taking on a new hobby. For me, that is where competing in triathlons started. It was something new. It pushed my elasticity well beyond where I thought I could go, allowing me to become a better and more flexible version of myself. But as I got deeper and deeper into this unique and special world, I began to learn several unexpected lessons. They ranged from how I could push my body and mind further than they could ever go, to the tricks of the trade that save you valuable time on the course, like some silly laces that don't require you to tie them.

These lessons, some small and some much larger, have translated to my life off of the racecourse. They have opened my eyes to new opportunity and perspective, expanding some of the limitations I perceived and replacing them with an attitude that I can do anything and succeed in any endeavor. That, in and of itself, is worth its weight in time-saving tricks. So, take a moment to ask yourself whether you are elastic. Are you flexible? Do you allow yourself to stretch and expand? If not, do so. Find something that challenges you, and go after it. Real adventure begins at the edge of your comfort zone.

Key Takeaways

- Small adjustments can deliver significant results.
- Being elastic, or flexible, can make a big difference.
- Real adventure begins at the edge of your comfort zone.

THE MECHANICS
OF THE MACHINE

MACHINES ARE EVERYWHERE. In our modern-day world of tech-nological advances, it would be nearly impossible to go even one day without the influence of a machine. Had coffee this morning? In all likeli-hood, a machine made it. Drove to work? You enjoyed the innovations of a machine we call a car. And, of course, used your cell phone? Well, that's probably one of the most important machines we possess. A machine is nothing more than a system or device that performs or assists in the performance of a human task. It usually has several working parts, or components, each with a definite function.

I have always been infatuated with watches. In watchmaking, a remarkably technical trade, the watchmaker assembles nearly microscopic component after component to mechanically work together and produce technical movements that tell time. Many high-end luxury watches are comprised of thousands of small pieces, and if even one malfunctions or is missing, the machine won't work. It is fascinating to think it takes hundreds of springs, coils, and movements to just display time, but that is what makes this little miracle of a machine so special.

As we start to think about performance and sport, especially endurance competitions and mountaineering, we can easily see why it is so common for athletes and participants to compare their bodies to a machine. Each part—the muscles, tendons, ligaments, blood, organs, and so much more—works together to ensure the machine churns and burns, producing the desired results. The better the machine and its working parts, the more likely we are to reach the finish line or summit.

If we look at our bodies, it is easy to consider not just each component that influences our mechanics but also the three essential components of our existence: the mind, body, and spirit. Each of these pieces of your existence form your essence or your life. If even one is out of balance, you won't have a chance to perform at your highest possible level. That is why, at least in part, it is so beneficial and crucial to understand the mechanics of the machine.

In racing terms, we often look at a bicycle, which we ride for at least two-thirds of a triathlon, as a machine requiring substantial mechanics. This machine carries us over the course of a 112-mile bike ride. Competitors invest thousands of dollars and hours and hours of their training to ensure they have the right machine for the race. They then focus on ensuring that the machine is expertly fitted for their bodies, focusing on every adjustable element to guarantee that they have a customized and comfortable experience. Even more impressive, each racer adjusts their bike—and/or their body—in a different way. Some prefer the seat to be higher, others the aerobars to be closer, while still others perform a slight bend of their leg rather than a more substantial one.

The goal? To position the machine in a way that allows for optimal power output and performance. It is truly amazing to see how much goes into creating an optimal biking experience. It also goes to show, as an example, the tremendous value we see in the mechanics of the machine. To be off even an inch here or there could make the difference between 112 miles of agony or comfort, between pumping your legs just a little bit faster and crossing the finish line just a little bit quicker. Mechanics means everything because machines rely upon it. Mechanics is a simple concept to understand but a hard one to execute.

In nearly all aspects of our lives, the hardest thing to do is to create motion. Energy manifests as motion, and motion manifests as progress. The more motion we create, the more we move in the direction of our goals. It is cyclical, and you need one to have the other. We can then build momentum, which will inevitably sustain our growth and success. When it comes to business, I never really thought about my success in terms of building a machine and then considering the mechanics that support it. However, participating in triathlons really shifted my paradigm to look at things on and off the course in different ways. I learned the value of excelling in different disciplines and ensuring that each and every component of the machine is in proper working order, highlighting the mechanics of each.

But as I compare triathlons to running a successful business, I can see just how closely related they are. In business, good mechanics help you build the right teams and generate the best possible processes and practices to support your deliverables and satisfy your customers. First and foremost, everyone from the CEO to the management team to your various departments are all part of your mechanics of success. Your teams are the most important parts of the machine, and it is crucial to have the right teams in place and the right members on each team. Having proper and scalable procedures and processes in place is the oil that's going to keep each part of these machines working properly. You need a whole bunch of other things to sprinkle in. Effective communication and transparency across the board are just two examples of what's going to also help ensure that each of these parts are working to their maximum ability.

Second, you are only as good as the weakest part of your machine. For example, swimming was always my shakiest discipline. Other than not fearing the water, I didn't have a particularly strong acumen for an efficient swim stroke, and I often found myself struggling just to finish the lengthy swim. However, I worked hard on my mechanics to ensure that I could successfully navigate the swim, and then I leaned in on my ability to run and cycle. These two pieces of the trifecta lifted my performance and allowed me to pick up the most time. However, that experience inspired me to think about the value of each part of the machine. Even one weak part can destroy your overall productivity and ability to reach your goals.

Think about your mechanics for a minute, both personally and professionally. Is every component aligned and working together for your own personal betterment? Are you displaying and exhibiting good mechanics in executing on each area of your life? I have found, at least in my own life, that there is always a great deal of work to do. You are lucky if you have all the right components in place. Few people do. Often, something is missing. Perhaps you are physically fit but are mentally destructive and unhealthy. Maybe you are mentally strong but lack any real semblance of a relationship with a higher spirit.

In each of these examples, you are missing an essential component to find balance. However, if you put in the work, you will likely have all the right components to make the machine run. Then the conversation turns to one of balance, which is where your mechanics come into play. It is crucial to ensure you are a well-oiled machine in your personal and professional life, which is not always easy. Your mechanics are your execution, where you decide how to allot your time and energy. Do that right and you will move forward, progress, and gain valuable momentum that will ultimately push you toward your goals and dreams.

Mechanics are a funny thing. They can be extraordinarily technical and easily unbalanced. Think back to that bike ride. As you navigate a large and graded hill, it is essential to rely on your leg strength but also the bike gears. Adjusting the gears will help you churn enough force to make it to the top of the hill. However, if you find yourself in the wrong gear, you have a higher likelihood of frying your legs and burning out.

This happened to me during IRONMAN Austria. My rear derailleur, which is a fancy word for a bicycle gear shifter, was somehow damaged while I dissembled, shipped, and reassembled my bike for the race. The malfunction didn't rear its ugly head until approximately fifty miles into the bike course, leaving me with only four of fourteen gears to work with through the hilly Austrian countryside around Lake Worthersee. The mechanics that should have ensured that I was pumping my legs at the right cadence by using the machinery of the bike to properly propel me failed, resulting in a longer than expected bike leg, severe cramps, and a very painful marathon run afterwards.

It is no coincidence that the two are so intimately related. Machines and mechanics, mechanics and machines. Deepak Chopra said, "Within every desire is the mechanics of its fulfillment." His words embody the beauty of mechanics. They are the blueprint for your success, the roadmap to help you fulfill your greatest dreams and desires. If you haven't considered your mechanics until now, start thinking about how they support you and keep you upright—or how they might otherwise stand as an obstacle on your path to great things. Luckily for us, it is not particularly difficult to change our mechanics. We can do so with just a few simple adjustments, if only we know what isn't working for us in the first place.

Your body, and your life for that matter, are machines. They are comprised of thousands of tiny components that influence everything you do. Your mechanics are how well your machine runs. Together, they are the tools you need to compete in a triathlon, summit a mountain, run a successful business, and navigate this complicated experience we call life.

Key Takeaways

- Make sure each and every component of your machine is in proper working order.
- You are only as good as the weakest part of your machine.
- Mechanics can easily become unbalanced. Maintain your machine so that it runs well.

DNF
(DID NOT FINISH)

IF YOU ARE A RACER, there isn't a more feared trio of words than "did not finish." These three seemingly harmless words can be the difference between success and failure, reaching your goals and falling short. The same is true in nearly everything you do. I can say from firsthand experience, nothing is worse than falling short. I remember one of my greatest racing failures like it happened yesterday. It was 2020, IRONMAN Cozumel in Mexico. As I mentioned earlier, although I was accepted to compete in the IRONMAN World Championship in Kona, I needed to maintain my eligibility by competing and finishing one of their races each year leading up to the grand event. Even though they were being very flexible with the racing requirements due to the pandemic, I chose to compete in Cozumel. It is a beautiful, mostly undeveloped Mexican island in the Caribbean. Known for amazing diving, it is also home to a very flat but very tough race.

The south side of the island is particularly windy, which makes for a physically challenging bike segment of a triathlon when the wind is acting up. Race day was like any other, but you could sense that the wind was running hard. Biking against it the entire race, this normally flat course felt like a steep incline. I felt like I was carrying another person on my back, trying to cut through the windy racecourse and get to transition to start the run. The 112-mile bike leg was simply grueling, divided into three laps around a thirty-five-mile course. When I hit the south side of the loop, I felt like I was peddling in quicksand. I pedaled as hard as I could, but I could only go eight miles per hour.

The bike portion of the race is sandwiched between the swim and the run. Normally, during the bike ride, I begin to mentally prepare for the run. It is a time of peace for me. But on this particular day, I was sweating it out. On just the second loop, I began to question whether I would make it to the finish line. With each pedal and pump, my legs came closer and closer to complete failure. I experienced a steady decline, inching closer and closer to quitting. I held on the best I could. No matter how hard I tried to fight through the pain and the lactose crushing my legs, my body gave out.

Before I could even begin the third and final loop and then head to the final discipline of the race, I turned in my bib and called it a day. At that point in my racing career, I had never once quit. Me, DNF? NFW! As they say, you never forget the first time you throw in the towel. It was a horrible experience; one I won't soon forget. To make matters worse, I still had to complete one more race to maintain my eligibility for Kona.

As a seasoned racer, I go into most races confident that I will not only make it to the finish line but also race strong. The substantial training regimen prepares you and helps build your race confidence. So, for most, it is surprising when you fall short. But it happens. So many unexpected circumstances can impact a race. Your sneakers could cause blisters; your bike could malfunction; your nutrition and fueling could be off; the weather could be brutal, and don't forget the cramping. Any one of these unpredictable challenges could cause you to fall short.

This happens in business as well. Think of how many leaders or dreamers have fallen short of executing a business idea, or missed earnings expectations, or made a bad hire, or flopped on a product rollout, or, in a worst-case scenario, filed for bankruptcy or had to close the doors. I experienced this failure as well. As much as we planned and rallied around an idea, sometimes it just fell short. At times, we downright failed. You know it's funny, in some ways a DNF is just a natural part of trying. You can't have failure unless you try. As Wayne Gretzky said, "You miss 100 percent of the shots you don't take."

That said, our collective goal should be twofold:

1. Try to avoid the DNFs in life.
2. Respond to them when they do occur.

The best and only way I know how to avoid falling short of your goals is to prepare to reach them. You'll never get far if you don't organize, plan, and then practice. I only failed to reach the finish line in one of the many triathlons in which I competed because I meticulously prepared for each race. I got my body in the right physical shape. I studied the course, and I would rarely skip out on a day of training, even when it was just so easy to sleep in. In doing so, I firmly believe I avoided many DNFs.

However, even when you try your best, failure is a normal part of life. How we choose to respond to failure is, inevitably, what defines us.

For example, after my catastrophic race in Cozumel, I returned home to New Jersey and signed up for three full-distance triathlons for the following year. I knew I had to maintain qualification for Kona, and that if I didn't, falling short would have a lasting impact on me. You can't be 100 percent successful 100 percent of the time. No one does that. Due to COVID, World Triathlon Corporation gave me a pass on 2020 after I showed my paid race registrations to attempt to compete. But 2021 was going to be my last chance for one last finish before the main event in 2022.

As I mentioned before, my first of three attempts came in IRONMAN Wisconsin. I was already signed up for IRONMAN Maryland the following weekend and strongly considered doing both just for the bragging rights of completing two only six days apart. I came into the race a bit overconfident and undertrained, which in and of itself is a recipe for failure. The bike course at this venue once again proved very challenging, but I made it before the cutoff, or so I thought. Racking my bike, I started seeing volunteers tearing down the transition tent, but I was comforted to see that the course wasn't closed yet and I would be allowed to continue to the marathon.

Knowing I had spent over eight hours on the bike course and cognizant of the allowed overall time limit, I knew I would have to get in a decent marathon time to claim an official finish. With tired legs, I gave it my all and crossed the finish line with plenty of time to spare before the midnight cutoff. My buddy was waiting for me in the finishing area. When I saw him, I pumped my fists and yelled, "Kona!, Kona!, Kona!" I had finally met the final requirement. As he helped me collect my bike and gear from the transition area, I was limping and hurting pretty bad. Pumping out a sub six-hour marathon on fried legs after a very tough bike race, I said there was no way I would race Maryland next weekend. "I'm in a lot of pain right now," I said. "I don't need the bragging rights."

Later, in the hotel, we were enjoying a beer when I logged on to the mobile app to check on my splits. I was mortified to see a DNF next to my name. Turns out that I didn't make the personal bike cutoff time. I missed it by ninety seconds, and I would not be given credit for the race. What I did make was the overall bike course cutoff, which is why I was allowed to continue, but I didn't make my individual cutoff, which is 10.5 hours after the start of the swim.

After the initial shock wore off, I turned to my friend and said, "I guess I'm going to Maryland next weekend." It worked out just fine as my wife and I got to visit a great town, Cambridge, and yet another race venue. Despite being bit by jellyfish as soon I entered the water, I had a good race and finished, really finished, and officially secured my Kona spot. How I completed that race over one hour faster than the one I did only six days prior is a testament to what the body and mind are capable of.

Ever heard of the professional boxer Evander Holyfield? He won the World Heavyweight Championship belt four times. You know how he did that? He first lost it three times. Evander is a great example of someone who knows how to make a comeback. One must recognize that failure is part of living and how you bounce back from it is the most important thing.

Sometimes, failure can really be a good thing. I have visited Alaska twice to try to summit the great mountain Denali. With six million acres of wild land, culminating in North America's tallest peak, Denali offers 20,310 vertical feet of pure intensity. When measured from base to summit, Denali is even taller than Mount Everest. It is a beast of a mountain, and I have tried to get to the top twice. On my first try, we lived at a 14,000-foot camp for two weeks waiting for a good weather window. It didn't come, and we couldn't even attempt to summit it. It was just too unsafe. As you can imagine, the companies that guide you to the summit are very careful and thoughtful about everything that could go wrong. Those who did reach the summit that week did so while traversing extremely life-threatening conditions. Meanwhile, without that same achievement under our belts, we left somewhat bummed.

However, I tried again a few years later. That experience was nearly as much of a letdown as the first. This one was on me though. I trained thoroughly and really thought I was ready, but the mountain proved me wrong. I was physically hurting at the end of each day, and it was clear. The guides kept encouraging me, and I persevered to continue to ascend to higher and higher camps. I kept going. Each morning brought on a new perspective that the worst was behind me and I could pull this off, but the guides were clearly keeping an eye on me.

Climbing up from 14,000 feet to 17,000 feet was the single hardest day of my mountaineering career. The guide was ready to turn me around halfway through that day, but I promised him I could make it and I did. But that would be my max altitude for this trip. The lead guide insisted that I wasn't going to join the rest of the group to attempt a summit and risk my health. If something had gone wrong, I could have returned with pulmonary edema at best or in a body bag at worst. So I took a DNF and waited at high camp for my team to perform their summit bid. As I waited in my warm sleeping bag inside a wind-sheltering tent, I saw what looked like ants going in the wrong direction down from the summit ridge. They had to turn around, again because of the weather. No one made it to the top that day, but everyone lived to return home and see their families.

The point is that sometimes a DNF can be a blessing. It is not always the worst thing in the world. In my experience, some of these DNFs saved my life. Who knows what might have happened if I had kept on trying to summit Denali? I may not have made it to the top, and I may not have made it back to the bottom or home. Failure may not always build character, but it certainly builds knowledge. The more familiar you become with any experience, the better you will be at managing it when it occurs again. Sometimes, small and repeated failures build your muscles to the extent that you can weather a much larger challenge or obstacle. In knowing that you can respond, you are armed with the ability to see clearly and navigate the difficult road ahead.

Thousands of examples exist of people who failed but eventually finished. I am one of them. So is Colonel Sanders in coming up with a recipe for his delicious chicken, and Thomas Edison in his efforts to create the light bulb. Remember the Japanese proverb, "Fall down seven times, get up eight"? This all starts with your mindset. We are all empowered with strong minds, the ability to manifest anything and everything that we want. However, we must literally put our minds to it.

Over the course of my many failures, I learned that not finishing is not failing. It is just not finishing. Nothing more and nothing less. Failure is falling short of your goals and never endeavoring to go after them again. Change the way you look at a DNF. We are all going to experience these in our lives. Assuming, of course, we are trying to live. Remember that you are the one in charge here. No one else. Hold yourself accountable when you fall short, and learn from the loss. Dust yourself off, and then move on. Simple as that.

It is easy to blame others when you don't reach your goals. I cannot tell you how many times I see a leader point fingers at his team for the shortcomings of his business. You want to talk about failure? That's failure. The jockey shouldn't blame the horse. An athlete shouldn't blame the bike. The leader shouldn't blame the team.

You are not your DNFs. Rather, you are a culmination of all the learning experiences you've had when you fell short. The finish line is ever elusive, and sometimes you just won't be able to get there. Trust me, I feel your pain. You are not alone. Take a walk in the streets of your neighborhood. Do you know what every person you pass has in common? They have fallen short of their goals. The difference, in your (and their) success and real failure, is how they bounce back.

Reaching the top of the mountain can be a difficult and tenuous journey, but your arrival makes it worth all the effort. What do you want your legacy to be? A quitter? A failure? Or someone who dusts themselves off and continues to fight? The decision, as you can imagine, is easy.

Key Takeaways

- Avoid falling short of your goals by preparing to reach them. You'll never get far if you don't organize, plan, and then practice.

- Sometimes a DNF can be a blessing. It is not always the worst thing in the world.

- Failure is a natural part of trying. Failure is part of living. How you bounce back from failure is the most important thing.

- Not finishing is not failing. It is just not finishing. Nothing more and nothing less. Failure is falling short of your goals and never endeavoring to go after them again.

THE EXIT MARKETPLACE

EXIT

Noun

—A way out, especially of a public building, room, or
passenger vehicle.

—An act of going out of or leaving a place.

Verb

—Go out of or leave a place.

ONE OF MY FAVORABLE EXITS, or summits, from my mountaineering adventures happened on Mount Kilimanjaro. Known as the Roof of
Africa, the trek up the mountain wasn't particularly technical but it was
challenging nonetheless. After a week of ascending and acclimatizing
over and over we finally made it to Barufu High Camp for a summit bid
the following day. At this point there was less oxygen in the air than in

all the previous days and our bodies and minds were tired. With labored breath while going around a bend, I saw the exit of the climb materializing in the form of the rustic wooden planks on Uhuru Peak symbolizing the summit at 19,341 feet above sea level.

My father had just passed a month before, the day prior was Yom Kippur, and I was unable to fast as per Jewish custom due to the high calorie requirements of the expedition. These thoughts combined with the sense of accomplishment of reaching 19,341 feet above sea level brought tears to my eyes for the final hour of this exit/achievement.

Most of us exit something each and every day. It could be as simple as walking out of a door to your office or your home or just leaving a room. In the traditional sense, we are always exiting something. But exiting means so much more, especially when it comes to the business world. I will never forget the day I fully left Binary Tree. It was the culmination of over two decades of ups and downs, blood, sweat, and tears. But in the end, that exit proved to be life-changing and incredible.

To me, and in the nontraditional sense, exiting is something special, a coveted goal that entrepreneurs desperately search for. It is also something that denotes completion or finishing something you started, like finishing a race, summiting a mountain, completing a project, or reaching a desired goal. When I started writing this book, I didn't have the faintest idea if I would ever get to the end. But here we are, one chapter to go, and I can sense the exit ahead.

In a more difficult sense, sometimes an exit can signify an end to something. Relationships often end with one partner exiting. You might find yourself unhappy in your current profession or career and decide to exit it. So, the act of exiting can be demonstrative of loss or ending, but it can also open up the doors for greater opportunity. It may be a painful endeavor at first, but suffering through that change can bring you to the doorstep of a brighter future. In short, the act of exiting can mean so much to so many. On this topic, *Necessary Endings* by Dr. Henry Cloud is one of my favorite books, which I highly recommend.

The exit marketplace, to me, is where we live. It is where change occurs. It is where fresh and new beginnings live and where moving past adversity resides. We have all seen a friend or a loved one who is simply unhappy in their present circumstances. We may tell them, again and again, it is time for change. What we are really saying is, "Get off your ass and move on from the thing that is making you unhappy." They likely agree with us but can't find the right words, or they struggle to put one foot in front of the other. This type of exit, as obviously helpful as it may seem, isn't an easy one to make.

In life, we are gifted with control. As human beings with developed brains, we are empowered to make decisions and take actions that influence and often dictate our circumstances. We can enter and we can exit nearly anything. External factors surely impact our present circumstances, but in reality, we have the power to dictate the end; we have the authority to make the decision to enter and to exit. It is wonderful to consider that no one, and I mean no one, can stop us. Barbara De Angelis said, "No one is in control of your happiness but you; therefore, you have the power to change anything about yourself or your life that you want to change."

Your circumstances, good or bad, begin and end with you. We create these positive environments and surroundings through practicing a few core concepts. The first is personal discipline, which is the ability to control your feelings and overcome weaknesses. It is the ability to pursue what you think is right despite temptations to abandon it. Now, this is not an easy muscle to develop. It can take time, some pain, and a relentless desire to power through. Yet, amazingly enough, we can navigate and traverse so much through being disciplined and dedicated to our goals.

The second core concept is to remain focused. Often, shiny objects distract us, making it difficult to concentrate and apply our energy and attention to our greatest and most important goals and undertakings. It is only natural for us, as humans with many interests and stimuli, to give our attention to numerous aspects of our lives. Rarely is it possible for us to sit down and devote 100 percent of ourselves to one task, one person, one platform, and one agenda. Unfortunately, we then get pulled in many directions and cannot give one goal our entire focus.

The final core concept is awareness. We are only as good as our understanding of our circumstances. Call it your environment or your habitat, but the more aware of and receptive to your present conditions you are, the greater the opportunity you will have to ensure your conditions support your healthiest and best life. Often, we lack awareness because we numb our pain or hide behind a content façade. That prevents our senses from alerting us to problems. The more we feel, the greater awareness we have, the likelier it will be that we'll be able to assess our personal culture and adjust accordingly.

These three core concepts—discipline, focus, and awareness—shape our ability to recognize our current state of being and determine what serves us the best and what we might otherwise want to change. The more we dig into these thoughts and feelings, the better positioned we will be to reach our goals, dreams, and desired exits.

As you are aware, I have been competing in endurance sports and mountaineering for more than ten years. As monumental as these events often feel when you are training for them or participating in them, the reality is that these are fixed moments in time that have a beginning, a middle, and an end. You exit through the finish line or summit, indicating the end or the achievement of a tremendous accomplishment. That is life in its purest form. We start and we finish. We exit and begin again. As we achieve, we find more to achieve. That is the nature of the world in which we live.

Recovering from a triathlon is an unbelievable ordeal. After a race, your body is completely broken down. Medically speaking, the human body experiences fourteen years' worth of deterioration after this 140.6-mile competition. Muscles fatigued, aches and pains running through every fabric of your existence, you are in desperate need of rest. Fortunately, the amazing machine that is the human body totally recovers and rebuilds all that is broken, and in the moments and days after getting to the finish line, you likely experience a moment of true clarity and appreciation for what you just accomplished. The same is true in nearly anything of meaning. The exit is a beautiful thing. In some ways, it is epic. Pure elation. Joy. In other ways, you are mourning the loss of something, navigating the pain of recovery, learning how to live differently.

In either sense, they are both integral parts of the circle of life. The exit should be felt and appreciated. Celebrate the exits; each one is a period on a sentence. An exit is the closure to the journey. However, often we complete one thing just to look for another. We rarely pause, look at the breadcrumbs we followed to get to that point in the road, and truly consider how we got there. But we should.

I have entered and exited so much of my life. In fact, I think we all have. You can't live without beginnings and endings. How we respond to these novel experiences can shape our futures. When I originally thought about this chapter, the exit marketplace, selling Binary Tree came to mind. But as I unpacked the concept in even greater detail, I came to understand that the exit is so much more. It is really about *starting and finishing*, which I think of as three of the most important words in the English language. Robin Sharma said, "Starting strong is good. Finishing strong is epic."

An entrepreneur's greatest dream is to build something that matters, eventually finding a path to monetize their dreams and hard work. To do that, though, is a long and arduous process. It is also a function of a number of crucial components—a good idea, a strong vision, significant dedication, and of course, a team willing to support you along the way. You need the right team members, subject matter experts, lawyers, accountants, and nearly every type of professional you can imagine. When you decide to exit, you then must compile a team of qualified financial advisors, that would also include an investment banker to help value the business and bring it to market. So many pieces to consider.

Once you agree to sell your business, which in hindsight was the easy part, and you get an acceptable offer, you then move into the due diligence portion of the show. Watch out for that! You'll never feel more intricately examined or scrutinized. It is like a trip to a doctor to get your annual physical—no stone goes unturned. This can last for upwards of six months, and every day seems to bring additional challenges. In the case of Binary Tree, we secured a letter of intent to close in six weeks. I couldn't believe it, and many professionals on my extended team told me it was the fastest closing process they've ever been part of. I attributed that to our philosophy of always closing our books, and ensuring we had our ducks in a row.

When our buyer asked us to present our financials, along with hundreds of other records, we were really quick and ready to spring into action. There were still hiccups, as there are in most due diligence processes. But, for the most part, things went according to plan. We were well positioned to rectify any issue that stood in our way, and made it to the finish line. For an event you dream about over the course of your entire life, it is actually pretty anti-climactic. Sitting there, in a large virtual conference room, you're not sure what to expect to feel like during this life-changing moment. Then you sign on the dotted line, and poof, you just traded your life's work for a bunch of cash.

For me, personally, it was strange to go from running my business in multiple capacities to literally being retired overnight. I went from going to the office, physically or virtually, every single day of the week, staying there well into the evening, and constantly managing my team, to waking up with no specific job or responsibilities. It was like a scene from a zombie movie, where the world is totally bare and everyone has fled an otherwise busy city. There were no more meetings, no more phone calls, and there was nothing on my calendar. I no longer had access to my email, systems, or my staff. I had loved my company, my baby, for so long. But, even though everything was eerily quiet, I knew it was time to move on. And that's the way I orchestrated my exit.

My favorite motivational poster hangs in front of my treadmill and indoor bike in my home gym. It reads: "You are judged not by what you start, but by what you finish." Somehow, reading those wise words by Jim George makes each hard workout that much easier. Who doesn't want to live an epic life? We all do. That begins with dedicating yourself to finishing what you started. To ensure you exit, even if the exit isn't exactly how you predicted it. Your drive, energy, and dedication to the cause keep you moving one foot in front of the other, and this elevates you to something special. Don't fear the exit. Embrace it!

Key Takeaways

- The exit marketplace, to me, is where we live. It is where change occurs. It is where fresh and new beginnings live and where moving past adversity resides.

- Create positive environments through personal discipline, focus, and awareness. These three core principles help us recognize our current state of being, determine what serves us the best, and identify what we might otherwise want to change.

- For entrepreneurs, or anyone wanting to lead an epic life, the focus isn't on just starting or finishing. It's about finishing what you started.

BEEN THERE, DONE THAT, WROTE THE BOOK

IT HAS BEEN AN AMAZING JOURNEY, but in some ways I am just now entering the most exciting part of my life. From post-business exit, to completing the IRONMAN World Championship, being in the midst of training for more endurance races, and watching my children develop and grow, there is little in my life that I'm not appreciative and enthusiastic about. As I continue to grow and evolve, it is remarkable to learn more and find my rightful place in this world. Even so, I feel like I am at a point where I can look back and assess all that I have done and can now give back by helping others along a similar path.

From the perspective of my business, it was tremendous to build an internationally recognized brand, a successful company that offered products and services to customers all over the world. Binary Tree employed more than two hundred employees across twelve countries at the end of its twenty-six-year existence, with hundreds of others spending years of employment there. In thinking about the wonderful people I met and worked with, it feels so good to know that many of them were around for the majority of the ride and exited the company with tremendous experience, creating many options for them in the market. Together, we built a preferred place to work, a strong culture, and a business that kept them coming to work day in and day out, giving it their all and working toward our collective goals.

From a personal perspective, I am lucky to have an incredible wife and two beautiful daughters. These two young ladies are quickly growing into strong, smart, and able women, and I watch in awe as they accomplish so much. My passion for adventure has rubbed off on both, and one races marathons and is embarking on a triathlon journey of her own. I am fortunate they'll still hang out with me. Larisa has given me thirty-two wonderful years of marriage, and I know there are at least that many more to go. Her constant cheerleading and wise counsel keep me grounded and help me navigate an otherwise strange world out there.

Much of my journey, at least the remarkable parts, seemed to have occurred later in my life. I didn't start racing as a young man. Well, young enough to still have some miles left on these wheels. But even so, most people don't wake up in their forties and say, "I am going to be an IRONMAN." That is precisely what I did. That may be one of my greatest accomplishments. Most people take the one and done approach to racing. However, I became a total addict. Endurance races are not for everyone, but they do build a tremendous amount of resilience and train your body to accept the challenge of going much farther than your mind could imagine.

Endurance races and adventures have become a way of life for me, my longest-lasting hobby. I intend to continue to race for years to come, even having just completed the landmark race in Kona. In many ways, racing keeps me honest. Until I started training, I am not sure I really knew what it meant to exhibit dogged and unfettered discipline, the type of stick-to-itiveness that spans nearly every second of every day. You don't get days off, at least not that many. There were days and days and days when I didn't want to get out of bed and train. But my mind would not falter, and it constantly pushed my body to do what had to be done. I am forever grateful for that grit.

They say it takes sixty days of willpower to build a habit. While that may or may not have been the case for me, I can share with you that eventually, along my journey, what felt like doing my homework turned into something that just became part of my life. Running ten miles, biking fifty miles, or swimming two miles began to feel as central to my existence as food, water, and oxygen. It was an automatic, a necessity, a definite. Putting in the work to build a habit is often the hard part, but for me, it became much more palatable each and every day. As human beings, we can form good habits or bad ones. I believe it is just as easy to become a regular smoker or drinker as it is to go to the gym every day or eat a healthy diet. The choice is yours. Which one do you think will serve you best?

My intention is not to tell you whether you are partaking in good or bad habits but to remind you that just as I learned over the course of racing, our repeated behavior and practices form our lifestyles and routines. We are empowered to make the choices that serve our best interests and create the best versions of ourselves and our lives. You can build habits in thousands of ways, from writing down your goals, to tracking your daily behavior through journaling, to having an accountability partner. Each of these practices supports creating habits.

As you engage in these disciplines, your body will reward you with a small dopamine hit. Doing this again and again will almost certainly train your body to covet this chemical release. So, we continue ahead and repetitiously do it. Then, we form habits. I am so thankful I caught on early and trucked through those first sixty or so days to form habits that would serve my goals.

They say hindsight is 20/20, and there is ample opportunity to review your present circumstances if you only look back to the road that got you to this point. My journey and present state of existence is no different. I am thankful for a lot, but there is plenty I would change if given the chance. I try not to think about how I would have built Binary Tree differently. I am proud of our hard work and, of course, we exited that marketplace on top. Even so, we could have taken chances to focus more on recurring revenue-type products rather than project-based ones. That might have allowed us to better predict cash flow moving forward and not get stuck in a hamster wheel of always having to sell and close.

We could have taken on outside capital which would have allowed us to scale at a much more aggressive rate. However, building a bootstrapped business with zero outside investments was one of our greatest accomplishments, so much so that I am not sure we would have been as strong and nimble as we were had we done it another way. Trust me when I say I am not beating myself up over it, but rather that I feel it is always valuable to look back and see how you might have ebbed or flowed in response to certain challenges you and your team might have faced.

Looking back, I could have been a better leader. I cared about my team deeply, but I made many mistakes in hires and fires and leadership changes over the years. Some decisions prevented me from doing the best for me, my family, and for Binary Tree. There were ample opportunities to be more strategic, less tactical, and more business-focused in my decisions. I don't regret most of them, right or wrong, as all contributed to the evolution of the business.

As a triathlete, I wish I had focused more on the quality of my racing than the quantity. I am proud of my twenty-plus triathlons, but I didn't always give it my all. Sure, I got to the finish line in all but one of these races, but I know I could have competed harder, trained more, and worked to secure a better time. I got them done but I didn't get them done fast.

Looking back, I believe that pushing myself and my body each race would have generated better results over time. I was so content making it to the finish line that I allowed that goal to lead to a sense of complacency I wish I had washed out early on. It is not that I didn't take it seriously, it is just that I wish I had pushed harder along the way. I fell in love with the journey more than the destination, which prevented my full effort to reach further and become faster.

Looking ahead, there is so much more to accomplish. As I turn to the next part of my journey, I am excited to become a role model to not just my kids but also to the workforce and to other business leaders. I have been there, done that, and now have written a book as the culmination of the first part of my flight. My new habits, which I am developing daily, are providing advisory services to other entrepreneurs. You see, leading isn't easy. Building a healthy business is hard. But it is hardly impossible, especially if people around you have done it before and understand the pitfalls along the way. I learned the hard way, perhaps through the school of hard knocks. I don't regret this trial by fire, but there was a better way. While I benefited greatly from advisors and mentors, I could have done so much more earlier in my career. I don't want other entrepreneurs to experience those same pain points. There is no need. Suffering is optional.

I have dedicated myself to race faster, harder, longer, and more challenging distances, but maybe not in nearly as many races. There is no need to compete in another twenty triathlons in the next ten years. However, I am constantly reinventing habits and trying to push myself. To that end, I know, whether I like it or not, that focusing on shaving time and racing faster or farther must be my next goal. While I've had some strong races over the years, there is more to do. It is easy to rest on your accomplishments, especially when they are, generally speaking, significant. However, that is where complacency and stagnancy creep in. That's where we lose our edge. But keep pushing and you will keep growing. Whether you win or lose, you are evolving.

I am far from a perfect human. In fact, like each of us, I am a work in progress. I made nearly every mistake along the way. Like the time I spent $50,000 to produce a company commercial for a Microsoft event. I wanted to be front and center, seen and heard as a big-time player. So we produced a short film to blow Microsoft away. It was crass and reeked of arrogance and ended up being a poor representation of who we were as a company, not to mention I threw away the equivalent of a gold Rolex in the process. Looking back, that is one of many examples where I strayed from our core beliefs and who I was as a leader.

Those regrets are some of the biggest examples of where I strayed from the principles that helped me build my business and create a strong family unit. So long as I stayed close to what got me there, I knew that even my worst outcome would be palatable. For that, I am thankful. Trust in your gut, and the rest will fall into place. My upbringing, the lessons my parents instilled in me from a young age, and the immigrant mentality helped create a strong sense of purpose, value, and a moral compass that has served me well. I developed into a free-spirited young man who cared about doing good while being grateful for all the opportunities that came into my life.

More than anything else, life is about having fun. Thankfully, I have had a lot of fun over these first fifty-four years of my existence. There is much to be done, to be learned, to be experienced, and to be lived. I hardly know it all, but I know a significant amount to help others. I want to impart on you, the reader, that if you are not having fun, then you won't do a good job, and eventually, you will give up on the challenge. Fun is everything. To this day, I try to have a lot of fun. The rest will fall into place. I am certain of it.

Many years back, I ran a triathlon in New Jersey with my oldest daughter. I also have enjoyed running two New York City Marathons and a half-distance triathlon with my youngest daughter. As I stood side by side with my children, watching them fight through their pain and experience race euphoria, I paused and truly realized the importance of the moment. I didn't want to leave them because I knew far too well that the bonk might be right around the corner. But they never did slow down, give in, or call defeat. In sharing the pain and joy of competition, I experienced an epiphany: I realized that I had accomplished all I set out to do. My children have the tools to compete, to train, to build healthy habits. They can do anything. As far as they are concerned, anything is possible.

Key Takeaways
Reflect on Your Life's Journey

I leave you with the following questions to help you determine where you are in life:

- Are you proud of your current state?

- Do you share your happiness and spirit with your friends and family?

- Do you feel joy on a daily basis?

- Is your career meaningful and purposeful to you?

- Are your relationships meaningful and mutually beneficial?

- What is your next finish line? Are you getting all the help possible to get there?

- If you could change even one thing about your life, what would it be?

Sit with these questions for a few moments. Think about your answers. Write them down. In contemplating and then answering these questions, you will begin to unlock the keys to your future while respecting and understanding your past.

AFTERWORD

IT WAS STRANGE to write some of this book while I was experiencing the very events I was writing about. Most of my story benefits from the gift of hindsight, but there is also something to be said to simultaneously experience and describe my journey to Hawaii and competing in the IRONMAN World Championship. Nonetheless, that story could also benefit from the perspective I have now, months after the actual race.

I keep a blog at stevenpivnik.com that details some of the play-by-play of most of my triathlons, ultramarathons, and mountaineering trips and other adventures. When I first started this book, I thought I would repurpose most of that content. Instead, I decided to relive the moments and write from a fresh perspective. But since the IRONMAN World Championship was one of the main driving forces behind this project, I thought you might enjoy a detailed recap of my experience in Hawaii. So, here you go:

Everything about the IRONMAN World Championship was world class. I've raced at over a dozen venues; all are great; some are excellent, but this one tops them all. If you're a triathlon junkie like me and competing in Kona is on your bucket list, leave it on there and continue to strive to add this race to your list of accomplishments. Trust me, it will be worth the effort and time once you do.

It is also world class in terms of difficulty. The heat and winds are unrelenting. They make the 4,500 feet of elevation gain during the bike leg seem like at least double that. The fact that the top ten pro men finished in under eight hours in 2022 is a testament to their superhuman abilities. It's very hard for me to fathom that type of performance, much less doing so in such difficult conditions.

It made a huge difference to me to arrive in Kona a week prior to race day. My emotion kicked in as soon as my wife and I boarded the eleven-hour flight from New York. It was amazing to think I was soon going to be at the starting line of this prestigious event with the best of the best iron distance pro and elite age group triathletes from around the world.

Upon our arrival in Hawaii, the ride from the airport offered me a first hands-on view of the Queen K Highway and the notoriously hot lava fields through which I would be racing. That, plus finally seeing the pier on Kailua Bay as we entered town at sunset, sent shivers down my spine. We then turned onto the famed Ali'i Drive, home to the finish line. I was overwhelmed. I've watched this event annually on NBC Sports and have seen countless YouTube videos of this exact location. It was very emotional to be there in person to participate in the event.

I was supposed to get in a thirty-minute travel shakeout run when I arrived, but I was exhausted. After checking in to the Royal Kona Resort, my wife and I wanted to get some dinner. The luau we wanted to attend was sold out, so we went to the nearest restaurant and had the first of many delicious meals. Boy did that first Mai Tai hit the spot in settling my nerves!

Race day was still a week away, so I resumed my training plan on Thursday. A 5k run and a 1,400-yard swim was on the agenda. Officials instructed us not to touch the sea turtles nor hold onto the dolphins. That was surely unique to hear about a race venue. These are incredible sea creatures and the thought of seeing them during a swim sent excitement down my spine. The sight of them was truly majestic. The water was as clear as anything I have every swam in and the visibility was crystal clear down to the very bottom. The coral reef was full of gorgeous tropical fish that seamed unphased by us swimmers above.

Friday's workout was my favorite Moneghetti speed routine. I ran up and down Ali'i Drive, envisioning myself crossing the finish line over and over again. It was my first real exertion effort in the Kona heat and gave me a great taste of what was soon to come. Temps were in the eighties, but with humidity in the seventies, it felt significantly hotter. I got in five miles with an average pace of 8:46 min/mile (very fast for me) and must have lost at least five pounds of water weight.

Later that afternoon it was time to start playing tourist, so we drove up to Mauna Kea. The summit is the tallest point in all the Pacific and is the tallest mountain in the world. Because it starts at the bottom of the sea, at over 30,000 feet in height, it is taller than Mount Everest. It took just over an hour to get to the visitors center at 9,000 feet of elevation where a mandatory thirty minutes of acclimatization was required to help prevent altitude sickness. We passed through several cloud layers on the ascent experiencing near zero visibility on certain sections of the road.

After getting some off roading instructions from the park ranger, we continued up to the nearly 14,000-foot summit, which is home to some super telescopes and star and space observation equipment. Boy was it cold up there! Forty-three degrees Fahrenheit (six degrees Celsius) to be exact, but the views were spectacular. The steep descent required engine braking in second and third gear, as the actual brakes would burn out if we regularly used them. The ride back into town was made extra special with an incredible sunset from altitude.

Saturday started with the first of many stops at the official merchandise tents. I've accumulated quite the collection of branded gear over the years, but it is time for all that to hit the donation bin and to be replaced with IRONMAN World Championship branded versions.

Later that day I picked up my bike, which I shipped through a company called TriBike Transport. It was time to hit the Queen K Highway on it to see first-hand what all this lava field heat was all about. Based on what I've read, winds can blow up to thirty-five miles per hour and sometimes higher, and temperatures can exceed 100 degrees Fahrenheit due to the reflected heat from the lava fields and asphalt.

It was windy but not too bad during this twenty-mile training ride. But again, I sure got a real taste of what to expect come race day: intense heat. It was tourist time again on Saturday night, and we signed up for the famous excursion of swimming with the manta rays. After a beautiful sunset on the pier, it was on to an outrigger style canoe and off into the night to attract the rays to come out and play. I can write a full blog post on this experience alone. If you want more details, you can Google "swimming with Manta Rays Kona" to watch videos. Just wow! Spending the evening with ten-foot-wide sea monsters—what could be better?

Sunday morning started with another swim. I got in 1,500 yards with a stop midway by the famous coffee boat docked offshore. I don't drink coffee but when in Kona . . . There was also an easy thirty-minute run on the plan. Adrenaline took over and I hit it a little harder than I should have and clocked a 5k in under twenty-seven minutes at an 8:40 min/mile pace. Again, that is super-fast for me.

Monday's plan was a repeat of Sunday's. The bay was quite choppy and there were significantly more folks out which made for great race day prep. I only got bumped once though. It would be much more violent in the water come Thursday. No coffee boat came out that day.

After a 1,600-yard swim it was 9 a.m. and race registration was finally open. I beat the rush and it was super quick and easy to get my racing bib, age group swim cap, numbered bracelet, and gear bags. With registration complete, it was off to complete another quick run. I wanted to experience a section of the course called the Natural Energy Lab so we drove out there. Here's a description of the course by Chris Foster of triathlete.com:

> The Natural Energy Lab has the ugly distinction of being the worst thing at the worst time. After already flogging themselves for the previous 132 miles, athletes take a left-hand turn off the Queen K Highway into a bowl of heat. Completely exposed, and actually boasting some of the highest levels of insolation in the coastal U.S. (insolation is basically the strength of solar radiation that reaches the Earth), athletes enter The Lab at almost exactly mile 16 of the marathon. When they exit 3 miles later, they're rarely the same. NBC's TV announcers like to memorialize an athlete entering the Natural Energy Lab like they're entering the dark side of the moon.

My short 5k run out there was nothing short of brutal. Running in a frying pan is the only way to explain it. Once again, I was happy to experience it so I would know what to expect on race day.

On Tuesday, World Triathlon Corporation held their famous charity underpants run. Thousands flooded the short one-mile jog in their tighty-whities and many other incredibly creative versions. It was great fun to participate in. I represented my homeland and sported Ukrainian colors. You can find pictures of this on my blog at stevenpivnik.com.

After some more shopping it was time for one last touristy activity while on this island. We drove out to Sunshine Helicopters on the northern part of the Big Island. While we signed up for the volcano and waterfall tour, the poor weather conditions prevented our chopper from showing us red hot flowing lava. While that was disappointing, the waterfalls and views that we did see were spectacular.

Eighteen more miles of biking awaited me when we returned into town to finally finish the training plan! To complete the day, I found the Big Island Chabad House and attended Yom Kippur services for the holiest day on the Jewish calendar. I'm thankful for many things but at the top of the list is the Almighty who for some reason chose this path for me. Thank you!

There was nothing rigorous on the plan for Wednesday other than an easy ten-mile spin on the bike which I leisurely completed at 7 a.m. just to keep the muscles loose. A short swim and run were optional, but I chose to stay horizontal as much as possible other than gear bag preparation and drop-off along with my bike to the transition area.

After breakfast with my coach for last-minute advice, I met up with several of my friends and teammates from TMB Racing. I may be the not fast, not last guy, but these guys are all very fast. Each qualified the "legit" way by finishing other races at or near the top of their age group. It was awesome to be in their company.

The last task for Wednesday was an airport run to pick up an addition to my support crew. My younger daughter joined me and my wife in Kona and somehow after a very long day of travel had the energy to go out for a training run. I don't know where she gets it from. Now she can claim that she trained for the New York City Marathon on Ali'i Drive in Kona. That is pretty cool! We were missing our oldest who couldn't make it due to work commitments, but she was there with us in spirit.

We returned home that evening, and it was time to prepare for the race. I laid out all my gear on the kitchen counter, turning the mess into organized race bag piles. That was as stressful as always with the ever-nagging feeling that I was forgetting something. I always check and double and triple check my packing list before traveling. I then returned to the carbo-loading program with nothing else to worry about. This was the first time I didn't have pre-race jitters because I'd swam in the Kailua-Kona Bay and rode the Queen K Highway several times. The only thing left to do was to try to get some sleep, wake up at the crack of dawn, listen to the national anthem, swim 2.4 miles, bike 112, run 26.2 in near 100-degree heat and high humidity, and call it a day.

The 4 a.m. alarm was nowhere near as jarring as at other races because going to sleep early kept the jet lag (minus six hours) in near full effect. By the way—there is nothing to do past 9 p.m. in Kona, so this was not hard. We moved from a hotel which was a mile away from the start/finish into an Airbnb which was even closer. This made getting to transition very easy. Body marking was replaced with race number temporary tattoos included in the race packet—a real nice touch to further raise the level of the event.

The cheering started even before sunrise as you entered the tent to clapping welcome volunteers. The next stop was to drop off my personal needs bags before heading to the transition area on the pier for one last visit with the bike. Personal needs bags are ones that you access approximately halfway during the bike course and halfway during the run course.

Part of my nutrition plan during the race was regularly drinking a carb and electrolyte mix out of two water bottles I stored on my bike. I got a great suggestion to put something I would really look forward to in my PN run bag. I chose Mountain Dew. I figured I would be sick of the Coke and Red Bull from aid stations after 127 miles. After topping off my tires to 120 PSI, putting my first two bottles of water with nutrition on my bike, and filling the bento box with gels, I was unpleasantly surprised that they weren't allowing access to the bike and run bags. You could only access the bike bag after coming out of the water and run bag after completing the bike course.

In all the other races I've run, I put the items on my nutrition plan into these bags the morning of the race. In Hawaii, I didn't do it at gear check-in the day prior because I feared they'd spoil in the heat. Now I was stuck with several gels, eight stroopwafels, and a PB&J sandwich, which I planned on devouring after the bike race. In response, I ate half the sandwich just to get those carbs on board and stuffed the rest into my bike jersey that I was going to wear anyway under my swim skin. The extra bulk was not ideal but I'm not a fast swimmer to begin with and I didn't want to deviate from my bike meal plan.

As I walked past the section where the bike bag was hanging, I asked a volunteer if they could smuggle eight waffles into my bag. With a wink the response was, "Your doctor said you needed these in your bag?" To which I replied, "Yes, he doesn't want me to die." The volunteer said, with a smile on his face, "OK, since your doctor doesn't want you to die, give me those waffles, #1981." I love these volunteers!

With final transition setup complete at 6:15 a.m., it was off to the starting coral to await the national anthem. As it was performed, I thanked God and my lucky stars for getting me to the event I've been dreaming about for the last 157 months.

Shortly thereafter my race was almost over before it even began. Many folks stretch and get their blood flowing by air swimming. This monster of a man started a back stroke without looking behind him and I got whacked hard right in the face. One inch to the right and he would have Hit me in my nose. One inch higher and he would have hit me in my eye. He hit me HARD, but my cheek bone took the brunt of it. He started apologizing in a language I didn't recognize (ninety-one countries represented this year) and I gestured "I'm fine" and walked away.

The start cannon went off at 6:30 and the pros officially started the 2022 IRONMAN World Championship. Following the pros, us amateurs took off wave by wave based on our age group. I wasn't up for another hour. I killed the time by continuing my morning carb up with a final Clif Bar, gel, and bottle of Gatorade.

Instead of starting the 2.4-mile swim several at a time like in most races, here the entire age group swims out about a hundred yards and treads water for an in-water start. My age group was so large that it took several minutes to get everyone in the water and out to the start area. My official time began before I even got to the actual start. I didn't mind as I wanted to be in the back to avoid the turbulence. Being punched on dry land was enough violence for one day.

That strategy was short lived, as many of the younger, faster age groupers who went next swam over me. Fortunately, there was no further carnage. Other than that, swimming in this bay several times already this week made for a smooth start. I made it to the halfway point in forty minutes, which gave me high hopes for a decent swim split. Unfortunately, the current and increased chop on the 1.2-mile return killed that ambition.

Since I was in the second to last wave of the day and not one of the fastest swimmers, the lifeguards who were out in full force on paddle boards started gathering on the sides to see us slow pokes home. I knew I had enough time to make the two-hour-and-twenty-minute swim cutoff but the feeling of being tapped on the shoulder and being told otherwise did creep into my mind. Total swim time ended up being an hour and fifty minutes. This was thirty minutes slower than I hoped for, but that didn't faze me much.

I found out afterwards that the athlete tracker apps glitched for my wife and daughter tracking me. It showed me finishing the swim in under forty minutes and stuck in transition for a *long* time. My wife made her way down to the officials by the swim exit to try and check on me. I was happy to see her when I came out, and she was happy to see me in OK shape and not laid out in the transition tent.

I don't think I have any swim exit pics from other races with me smiling. I was beaming in that one, ecstatic to finally be out of the water after almost two hours. Being that this was Kona, I hammed it up a bit for the camera for the first time ever after the swim. There were hanging freshwater hoses right by the swim exit to rinse off the incredibly salty water and then it was off into transition to get my swim skin off and my bike shoes on. After a walk/jog across most of the pier, I found my bike with helmet attached and my wife and daughter on the other side of the fence cheering me on.

The anticipated and practiced Queen K Highway ride would have to wait as the first eight of the 112 mile bike course was in and around hilly Kailua-Kona. My legs weren't even warmed up yet and they were already being stressed. Then I was finally in anticipated territory and got down into the aero position to brave the legendary bike course through the lava fields.

The heat and winds were a force to be reckoned with, but relatively fresh legs and race adrenaline allowed me to average sixteen miles per hour for fiftyish miles until the climb to the town of Hawi began. I was hoping to average at least seventeen but was happy with sixteen considering the heat and cross and headwinds. The average came down to just over fifteen miles per hour by the time I hit the turnaround.

Right after that I was able to access my personal needs bags that had two more bottles of 400 calories and over 1,000 mg of electrolytes waiting for me. By then it was about 3:45 p.m. and the extreme heat had turned my upcoming liquid meal into hot soup. I had no choice but to take them in over the next hour. I was optimistic that the headwinds up to this point would be a welcome tailwind but there was no such luck.

The common buzz amongst athletes' post-race was how we all had to endure head winds both ways. Thanks a lot, Kona! Having to pedal hard even downhill to maintain a pace was not easy, and it was very mentally draining. It was definitely going to be a grind for fifty more miles but no one expected this to be easy. I was hurting but nowhere near done yet.

I have the utmost respect for my friends, teammates, and others who averaged over twenty miles per hour for this course. Kudos to your skills, strength, and ability! Maybe one day. As my average speed was very slowly but surely decreasing, I started having flashbacks to IRONMAN Wisconsin last year where I missed the bike cutoff by ninety seconds. I can redo Wisconsin whenever I want, but this was my one shot at Kona, so I continued to dig as deep as I could until a sign totally took the wind out of my sails.

"Bike cutoff 5 p.m." it read. Switching screens on my Garmin bike computer I saw that it was approaching 4 p.m. and I still had twenty-two miles to go. I cranked up my speed to twenty-two miles per hour and immediately knew that it would be impossible to maintain this for even five more minutes. That effort brought on some serious cramps in both legs simultaneously. Fortunately, I was able to deep breath them away.

I pulled up to the next rider ahead of me and asked what time the bike cutoff was. Officially it's 10.5 hours after you enter the water or a certain time of day, whichever comes first. His reply was "Hi, this is my first time Kona." Like I said, ninety-two countries. Pulling forward I posed the same question to the next rider I approached. He explained that the sign we just passed had a 5 p.m. cutoff and we were one hour ahead of that. I breathed a massive sigh of relief and continued to crank away.

It's well documented how extreme exertion depletes cognitive ability, so I stopped trying to do math and just pedaled as hard as my legs would allow. At mile 100 I started seeing a light at the end of the tunnel, but them cramps reared their ugly head again. Oh, how I love my new breathing secret weapon. They were gone as quickly as they had appeared.

I pulled into transition seven and a half hours after I hit the saddle. Sunburned and exhausted but rejuvenated by seeing my family and coach just after I dismounted and started walking/jogging my bike back to its spot. I grabbed my run bag, exchanged my bike shoes for sneakers, lubed up my feet to prevent blisters, donned a pair of running socks, replaced my bike helmet with a run cap, and it was off to complete a 26.2-mile run so I could claim a World Championship finish.

As disappointing (for me) as my swim and bike splits were, I still had seven hours to complete the marathon before the seventeen-hour cutoff. With running being my strongest of the three disciplines, I knew I had a sub-five-hour marathon in me regardless of how fatigued I was. As I started running, I remembered the sage advice I had received just the day prior from my good friend and two-time IRONMAN World Championship finisher Igor, which was, "No one asked Neil Armstrong how long it took him to get to the moon. He is known for just getting there."

After a quickish first mile, I slowed down and speed walked / jogged most of the run course. I knew I would be a hot mess and quite a chore post-race for my wife and daughter had I pushed my pace for the run. I wanted to savor the finish without hobbling and hurting, and to recover quickly so we could enjoy the rest of our time in Hawaii. I enjoyed the sunset, stared at the stars and moon, and let this all sink in over the next five hours. I must say, after twenty-plus marathons, this was the most special 26.2 miles yet.

I made a friend at the end and jogged the final five miles with him to cross the finish line at 11:19 p.m., with a total finishing time of 15:43:34. I did not beat my 13:01 personal record but it was far better than the 16:53 it once took me to finish. I didn't care one bit. I had officially finished the IRONMAN® World Championship to the welcoming words of retiring legendary announcer Mike Reilly bellowing, "Steven Pivnik, you are an IRONMAN!" over the mic.

What had contributed to this triathlon addiction thirteen years before was my younger daughter running up to me after I'd finished my very first sprint triathlon and saying, "I don't care how wet you are, I want to hug you, I'm so proud." As if scripted she ran up to me with outstretched arms and I yelled "No, I'm soaked!." Her reply was "I don't care!" as she hugged me. This was followed by hugs and kisses from my wife as I shed some tears and congratulations from my coach who was there too.

We all walked together to collect my finisher medal, hat, and T-shirt. After we took some pics, I got my bike to ship home, and it was back to the condo for a quick beer before some Advil PM and bed. We had a plane to catch at noon to start the vacation and celebration in earnest in Maui.

Mahalo and aloha, all!!

AUTHOR'S NOTE

DEAR READER,

I hope you enjoyed reading *Built To Finish* as much as I enjoyed writing it. If you did, it would mean the world to me if you would leave me a five-star review on Amazon.

Details and pictures of all the adventures mentioned in this book can be found at stevenpivnik.com/blog. Search for the race or mountain name to get more details about the event, along with many photos. If you're considering any of the events or adventures I've mentioned, I would love to answer any questions you have.

If you're having a challenge growing your business or are considering an exit, I can try and help. If you would like a motivational keynote speaker for an upcoming large group meeting or conference, I would love to hear from you. You are also welcome to drop me a note with any feedback you have. I can be reached via my website at stevenpivnik.com, or email me directly at steven@stevenpivnik.com. I apologize in advance for any delayed response—I'm probably out racing or climbing.

I wish you the best of luck in setting and achieving your life goals. You are built to finish!

With deepest appreciation,

Steven

ACKNOWLEDGMENTS

I AM TODAY a sum of all my experiences and all of the people that I have met along my journey. I can probably write a chapter on each of these people below. But, I will do my best to be concise, although each of these people deserve an entire book of gratitude.

First and foremost, to my grandparents, parents, and aunt: I have no words for the sacrifices you made to immigrate to the United States and for the opportunity you created for our family. Mom and Aunt Svetlana—I hope you enjoy the book. Dad, Grandpa, and Grandma—may you rest in peace. Please continue watching over us from above.

To my wife, Larisa: The words "thank you" never seem like enough for the love and support you provide on a daily basis. I'm sorry/not sorry for my past addiction to work and that my races and adventures seem never-ending, but so is my love for you.

To my daughters, Stephanie and Rochelle: Raising you is our greatest accomplishment in life. It is priceless to include you in my list of best friends. I am in awe of your drive and creativity. Know that I will always be by your side in support of your endeavors.

To my sister and my nieces: You guys are such an inspiration. From the bond that you have with one another to the drive that you show daily. Your accomplishments and entrepreneurial spirit are a testament to the very reason we left the former Soviet Union. Ang—I'm glad you didn't pursue the Cross Fit Championship, though it's great to see that the fitness-crazy gene runs deep in the family.

To my cousins: I'm very fortunate to have you in my life, and I'm grateful for the relationship we have, despite our age differences. Your kids are going to be forces to be reckoned with. Keep up the great work!

To my long list of friends: If I start listing names, I'll exceed my publisher's word count limit. I am wealthy beyond words in this category and beyond grateful. I'm still BFFs with folks from grade school and high school. I've picked up many others along the way, or I should say we picked up each other. They say it's tough to make close friends later in life, but I've disproved that, and I'm thankful for the incredible relationships I've established in my forties and even early fifties. I love you all.

To the employees, contractors, vendors, suppliers, partners, and customers of Binary Tree: Wow, what a ride! Thank you from the bottom of my heart. The thing that excites me most about the relationships we've established is the occasional ping I get with "When are you getting the band back together?" or "What's next? I'm In!" I don't have any specific New Co. plans right now, but never say never.

So many employees contributed to the success of Binary Tree. Listing them would add fifty pages to this book. Two stand out. Thank you Carl Baumann and Vadim Gringolts for your combined forty-plus years of blood, sweat, and tears by my side. Your hard work, dedication, creativity, and leadership paved the way for us to achieve the growth and recognition that we did.

I've had many advisors and business consultants along the Binary Tree journey, but a few deserve special mention:

Pam Singleton from The CEO Project: Thank you for recruiting me to join a CEO peer group that you ran. Your guidance and support were priceless, as was your shoulder to cry on during rough patches.

Jim Schleckser, founder of The CEO Project: Thank you for starting this incredible program, for your guest appearances in my group meetings, and for recruiting me to lead the next group of high performing CEOs for you. I'm flattered!

Mark Hodges, Bill Thomas, and John Lema from Acresis LLC: I love your tag line . . . "We speak founder." You sure do! Your advice and network proved priceless when it came time to scaling and preparing Binary Tree for an exit. I'm flattered to be working with you as well to help other entrepreneurs along a similar journey as mine.

Nick Wilkinson: Thank you for running my baby as its CEO. I am forever grateful for what you achieved, not to mention the time your presence gave me to focus on my endurance addiction and passion to get to Kona. I can't wait for your movie to be made and to play the role of one of the biking MAMILS (Middle Aged Men in Lycra).

Speaking of Kona and biking: I've had the pleasure of training with some incredible coaches and triathlon teams. Thank you Keith Cook for getting me across the finish line of my first IRONMAN Lake Placid and doing it faster than either of us expected. Thank you to Ray and Eve Campeau and all the friends I've made over the years at TMB Racing. I couldn't have made my personal record (again in Lake Placid, years later) of thirteen hours and one minute without your guidance and support. Also, thank you to Brad Williams and KIS Coaching for getting me ready and across the finish line at the World Championship in Kona. Thank you for taking my daughter under your wing for her NYC Marathon PR and to her first triathlon finish at IRONMAN 70.3 Maryland. Thank you

Angela from BestResults2Day for the excellent nutrition plans you've provided over the years. Lastly, thank you Matt from TrainDirtyLiveClean for all the strength training you've put me through.

Igor Yakushko: I've cherished our relationship ever since we met after completing IRONMAN Lake Placid in 2011. It is priceless to have a great friend, motivational and endurance coach, and nutrition guru all wrapped into one. Your constant "you should write a book" comments after each of my blog posts finally hit home. Looking forward to seeing you add to your thirty-plus finishes. I'm sure we'll do many more together as well.

I've made many other new friends since embracing the endurance lifestyle. I would inevitably miss a few names, so I won't list them. Just know that I appreciate our virtual chats, mutual encouragement, and training monitoring on Strava. I wish you guys the best in your ongoing racing and life pursuits.

Thanks to Justin Spizman for all your writing assistance on this project. You made it go much easier than I ever thought possible. It goes without saying that I could not have done this without you.

It takes a village to get a man to the top of a mountain. This project was as much of an endurance event as many of my adventures. I am grateful to the amazing team at Greenleaf Publishing. Thank you Jen Glynn, project manager; Lee Reed Zarnikau, senior editor; Jordan Smith, copyeditor; Aaron Teel and Alyse Mervosh, proofreaders; Teresa Muniz, cover designer; Jen Rios, marketing manager; Amanda Marquette, marketing strategist; Kristine Peyre-Ferry, distribution director; and Gwen Cunningham, media strategist. Listing names is always a gamble, so my apologies if I missed someone!

ABOUT THE AUTHOR

STEVEN PIVNIK is a serial entrepreneur specializing in the Information Technology market. He grew his last company, Binary Tree, to over two hundred employees across twelve countries before realizing a successful exit with a sale to Quest Software. Steven now advises other founders and entrepreneurs looking for a similar corporate growth and company sale journey.

While Steven was CEO of Binary Tree, the company was named to the Inc. 500 and Inc. 5000 list of fastest growing companies multiple times, including a stretch of seven years in a row. Steven was known not only for negotiating and closing multimillion-dollar licensing deals with the likes of IBM and Microsoft, but also for creating a corporate culture with significantly below-average employee turnover and above-average customer satisfaction ratings and an executive leadership team that sparked creativity and drove a passion for winning and success across the entire organization.

Steven is also an endurance sport enthusiast and enjoys triathlons of all distances as well as ultramarathons and mountaineering. He has competed in over twenty triathlons including the IRONMAN World Championship in Kona, Hawaii, eight New York City Marathons,

Ultraman Florida, and numerous ultramarathons including distances of 50k, 50 miles, 100k, and 100 miles.

Steven enjoys public speaking about his business and sporting adventures with the hopes of motivating others to follow in his footsteps. He can be reached at www.stevenpivnik.com.

When not traveling for work, pleasure, or adventures, Steven and his wife live in Manhattan.